Science

Preschool–Kindergarten

Great science activities and reproducibles from the 1997–2004 issues of *The Mailbox*® magazine

Fall Science	Winter Science	Spring Science	Anytime Science
• Trees	• Ice	• Butterflies	• Bubbles
• Acorns	• Winter Weather	• Living and Nonliving	• Sound
• Leaves	• Shadows	• Plant Parts	• Air
• Pumpkins	• Dental Health	• Insects	• Sink or Float

Plus 29 more science topics!

Managing Editor: Cindy K. Daoust

Editorial Team: Becky S. Andrews, Kimberley Bruck, Karen P. Shelton, Diane Badden, Thad H. McLaurin, Sharon Murphy, Karen A. Brudnak, Hope Rodgers, Dorothy C. McKinney

Production Team: Lori Z. Henry, Pam Crane, Rebecca Saunders, Jennifer Tipton Cappoen, Chris Curry, Sarah Foreman, Theresa Lewis Good, Clint Moore, Greg D. Rieves, Barry Slate, Donna K. Teal, Zane Williard, Tazmen Carlisle, Marsha Heim, Lynette Dickerson, Mark Rainey

D1561105

©2006 The Mailbox®
All rights reserved.
ISBN10# 1-56234-624-5 • ISBN13 #978-156234-624-9

Manufactured in the United States
10 9 8 7 6 5 4 3 2 1

Table of Contents

Fall Science

A Tribute to Trees

Use these tree-themed activities to capture the blossoming, budding wonderment of trees as your students honor National Arbor Day by creating this magnificent classroom display!

by Lucia Kemp Henry

"Tree-mendous"!
branches
leaves
trunk
roots

Get the Feel for It

Challenge youngsters to feel their way through this tactile activity using their "tree-mendous" problem-solving skills! In advance, place a twig, leaf, walnut, pinecone, and piece of bark into separate brown paper bags. Gather your little investigators and tell them that each bag holds a clue to what they will be studying. Invite a volunteer to close her eyes and place her hand inside a bag. Ask her to describe the shape and texture of the object and then guess what it is. Then have her show the object to the class. Continue in this manner with the remaining bags. Display all five clues and then ask for students' conclusions about the topic of study, leading them to "trees" if necessary.

Hug a Tree Today!

Embark on this hands-on activity that gets your little woodworkers up close to a tree! First, give each pair of students two six-inch squares of white paper and a piece of brown crayon. Then take your class outside to mingle with the trees. Ask each child to close his eyes, touch the bark of a tree, and describe to his partner what it *feels* like. Next, ask each child to open his eyes and describe what the bark *looks* like. Then ask one child in each pair to hold a paper square flat on the tree while his partner uses the side of the crayon to create a rubbing. (If you do not have access to real trees, share books with photographs or drawings of tree trunks, and have each child create his own bark design.) Have partners change roles and repeat the crayon-rubbing activity. Ask your youngsters to glue their bark rubbings onto a length of brown bulletin board paper to create a large tree trunk. Later, staple the top edge of the tree trunk to a bulletin board so the bottom edge touches the floor. Then tape the lower section of the trunk to the wall. Complete this model tree with the four activities on page 5. What a great way to spruce up your classroom!

Getting to the Root of It!

Down, down, down go the roots and up, up, up grows a tree! Show your little ones a picture of tree roots from a reference book. Ask them to describe what a tree's root system looks like and then point out where the thickest and thinnest roots are located. Discuss how the roots keep the tree from falling over when the wind blows and how they carry water to the tree's trunk and leaves. Then create a root system for your classroom tree. Give each of several children a length of brown crepe paper streamer to tape to the bottom of the tree trunk and onto the floor to represent the larger roots. Provide the remaining children with lengths of thick brown yarn to tape onto the streamers to represent the thinner roots. Remind students to watch where they step so they don't uproot their work!

Branching Out

Your budding tree experts will reach for the treetops as they create the branches for their tree model. Step outside with your class to observe the branches of a real tree. Explain that the branches give the tree its shape. Show examples of how the branches twist and turn. Return to the classroom and give each child a 1' x 2' strip of brown bulletin board paper. Demonstrate how to roll the paper into a tube, twist it into a branchlike form, and then tape it closed as shown. Then help each child roll, twist, and tape his paper. Finally, arrange and staple (or tape) the branches above the trunk. Your classroom tree is shaping up!

"Leaf" It to Us!

Top off this terrific tree with student-made leaves! Collect real leaves for your youngsters to observe. Ask each child to carefully look at a leaf and describe its color and vein pattern. Explain that the leaves make food for the tree. Next, make a construction paper copy of the leaf pattern on page 7 for each child. Have small groups of students sponge-paint their leaves green and then use green-tinted glue to add veins. When the paint and glue are dry, have each child cut out her leaf. Then staple or tape your youngsters' fabulous foliage to the branches of the classroom tree.

Finishing Touches

If desired, label word cards with the parts of the tree (trunk, roots, branches, leaves) and add them to the display along with the title "'Tree-mendous'!" Later, encourage your tree experts to tell you about each part of the classroom tree. Then allow your youngsters to stretch out as they dramatize "I Am a Tree!" on page 6. Trees are top-notch!

leaves

Trees Are Our Friends

Plant some respect for trees with this thoughtful activity. In advance, cut two large tree shapes from bulletin board paper. Label one tree "A tree is…" and the other one "A tree has…" Post the trees near the model tree created in the activities on pages 4 and 5. Read aloud the book *Be a Friend to Trees* by Patricia Lauber. Show the book's illustrations as you ask each child to suggest a word to complete the phrase "A tree is…" Write each response on the matching tree. Next, use the tree parts from "Get the Feel for It" (page 4) to prompt responses to the phrase "A tree has…" Write youngsters' comments on the corresponding tree. What a forest full of facts your students have cultivated!

A tree is…
green
big
beautiful

A tree has…
leaves
branches
roots

Let's Tell About a Tree

Reinforce what your tree lovers have discovered about their woodsy friends with this song. Have your students sing the first verse several times, each time finishing the verse with a different word from the "A tree is…" tree (see "Trees Are Our Friends" on this page). Then ask them to sing the second verse in the same manner, using words from the "A tree has…" tree. There's so much to tell about trees!

(sung to the tune of "The Farmer in the Dell")

Let's tell about a tree.
Let's tell about a tree.
We know about a tree;
We know a tree *is* [green].

Let's tell about a tree.
Let's tell about a tree.
We know about a tree;
We know a tree *has* [leaves].

I Am a Tree!

When your youngsters perform this action rhyme, they will really get a feel for what it means to be a tree!

I am a tree. These are my roots.
They help hold me up,
Like a strong pair of boots!

Stand tall and point to feet.
Place feet apart, toes pointed out.
Rise up and lower on toes.

I am a tree. My trunk is right here.
I'm dressed up in bark
In the front and the rear!

Stand straight; put hands on hips.
Pat legs and tummy with hands.
Point to chest; point to back.

I am a tree. My branches are wide.
They grow up and up
And sway side to side!

Stretch arms out to the side.
Stretch arms overhead.
Wave arms side to side.

I am a tree. These are my leaves.
They make cool, green shade
As they blow in the breeze.

Wiggle fingers.
Arch arms over floor in front of body.
Wiggle fingers and sway side to side.

Bookmarks

Nurture your child's budding interest in trees by sharing a good tree-related book.

A Tree Is Nice
By Janice May Udry

Mary Margaret's Tree
By Blair Drawson

The Magic School Bus Plants Seeds: A Book About How Living Things Grow
By Joanna Cole

Fun activities to celebrate trees!

- Prepare some tree treats for a snack, such as broccoli florets with dip, tree-shaped sugar cookies, or apple slices.

- Count the trees in your yard. Find the tallest tree and the smallest tree.

Nurture your child's budding interest in trees by sharing a good tree-related book.

A Tree Is Nice
By Janice May Udry

Mary Margaret's Tree
By Blair Drawson

The Magic School Bus Plants Seeds: A Book About How Living Things Grow
By Joanna Cole

Fun activities to celebrate trees!

- Prepare some tree treats for a snack, such as broccoli florets with dip, tree-shaped sugar cookies, or apple slices.

- Count the trees in your yard. Find the tallest tree and the smallest tree.

©The Mailbox®

Note to the teacher: Duplicate a bookmark for each child. Encourage him to color the bookmark and take it home to share with his family.

Investigating Acorns

When it comes to teaching science concepts, "nuttin'" beats these acorn activities!

ideas by Suzanne Moore

What Is It?

Crack into your acorn study with this intriguing inference activity. Out of students' view, place an acorn inside a clean, plastic margarine tub with a lid. During your group time, have students pass around the tub. Invite each child to gently shake and tilt the container to help him guess what is inside of it. Then provide students with a final clue by reciting the rhyme below. After each child has made a guess, remove the lid to reveal the acorn.

You can find them on the ground
Or growing on a tree.
Squirrels like to eat them
Or bury them, you see.

DID YOU KNOW?

Acorns are the *fruit* of the oak tree and are a favorite food for animals such as deer, birds, squirrels, and mice.

Note: After handling acorns, be sure both children and adults wash their hands thoroughly with soap and water.

Acorns Up Close

To prepare for this small-group activity, collect two empty margarine tubs and a supply of brown acorns. Then make a class supply of the recording sheet on page 10. Provide each child in a small group with a recording sheet. As a group, sort the acorns into two groups: with caps and without caps. Then have each child complete the two boxes on her sheet by drawing and counting the capped and uncapped acorns. Next, remove the caps from the acorns and then place the acorns in a plastic bowl. Pour water into the bowl until the acorns are completely immersed. Soak the acorns in the water overnight. The next day, have each child observe the acorns and complete the bottom of her recording sheet.

To prepare for a plant-an-acorn activity:

Discard any floating acorns. (Floaters may have been damaged or dried out.) Place the remaining acorns in a resealable plastic bag and refrigerate them for approximately one month. (This is believed to help ensure faster and more complete germination.) Then throw an acorn-planting party!

Read aloud *In a Nutshell* by Joseph Anthony.

Name _____

My Acorns

Sort.  Draw. Count.

Caps	No Caps
_____ acorns have caps.	_____ acorns do not have caps.

Count.

How many [acorn with cap] ? _____

How many [acorn no cap] ? _____

Draw.

Note to the teacher: Use with "Acorns Up Close" on page 9.

Wonders Never Cease

Simple Science for Young Children

"Unbe-leaf-able" Fun!

Rake together some scientific thinking with these hands-on leaf explorations.

by Leanne Stratton

Pile 'em Up!

Fall into your study of leaves with this activity. In advance, have students collect a variety of leaves and bring them to school on a specified day. Cut out three large paper leaves similar to the ones shown. Program the leaves with the corresponding edge type. Tape the leaves to the floor, leaving space between them.

Begin the activity by discussing the types of leaf edges. Have students inspect their leaves and compare them. Direct students to sort their leaves by edge type and pile them on the appropriate cutout. (Set aside leaves that don't match one of the three edge types.) Then have the class predict which pile contains the most. To check the prediction, encourage students to align the leaves under the cutouts and then count each type. Finish by having students record the results on a class graph. Leafy learning really piles up!

Did You Know?

The three main types of edges found on broadleaf plants are *smooth, toothed,* and *lobed.*

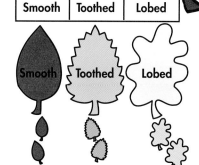

Smooth	Toothed	Lobed

Smooth	Toothed	Lobed

Investigating
Explaining

Sippin' Up Chlorophyll

Bet you'll see more than green thumbs when your youngsters explore leaf color changes with this hands-on model!

Materials for one:

2 white leaf patterns
clear tape
clear plastic cup

straw
serving of lime-flavored drink

Give each child two leaf patterns. Have her color one leaf green and one leaf yellow. Instruct each child to cut out the leaf patterns and place them back-to-back. Next, have her tape both sides of the cutouts together; then slide a straw through the openings at the top and bottom. Demonstrate how to place the leaf straw in the cup (green side out) and drink while slowly turning the straw to reveal the yellow side. Then invite each child to break down the chlorophyll in her cup (drink it) to reveal her leaf's true color. Yummy!

Did You Know?

The pigment *chlorophyll* is used to make food for the plant and gives leaves their green color. The chlorophyll hides the existing pigments in the leaves. In the fall, shorter days and cooler nights break down the chlorophyll, revealing the underlying colors in the leaves.

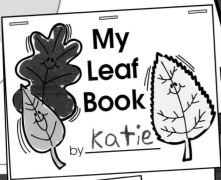

Observing
Defining
Communicating

Build a Leaf

Illustrate the different parts of a leaf by making these unique booklets with small groups of students! Gather the listed materials and then guide students through the steps below.

Materials for one:
leaf
copy of page 13
sheet of white copy paper (back cover)
three 5½" x 8½" pieces of transparency film
   (or laminating film scraps)
access to a stapler
black permanent marker
permanent marker in an autumn color

Steps:
1. Write your name on the line and then color the leaves on the front cover.
2. Cut apart the cover and text strips.
3. To make the back cover, fold the plain sheet of paper in half and then glue the top and one side's edges together to make a pocket as shown.
4. Stack the clear pages between the covers and staple along the top.
5. Glue text strip 1 to the back of the front cover at the top.
6. Glue each remaining text strip (in sequential order) to the back of a different clear page at the top.
7. Use a black permanent marker to trace the leaf's blade below text strip 1.
8. Keeping the leaf in place on page 1, turn the pages, tracing the veins on page 2 and the stem on page 3 and coloring the complete leaf on page 4.
9. Write the color of the leaf on the line on page 4.
10. Store the real leaf in the pocket of the back cover.

Did You Know?
Most leaves have three parts: the *blade* (the flat part), the *veins* (tubes that transport food and water in the leaf), and the *petiole* (similar to a stem).

Experimenting
Observing
Recording data

Fall, Leaves, Fall

You'll hit the bull's-eye with this nifty activity. In advance, prepare a chart and a large red and white bull's-eye target as shown. Place a variety of leaves, the chart, and the target in a center. Invite each youngster to choose a different leaf. Explain that he will be testing his leaf to see whether the leaf twirls, falls fast or slow, and lands on the target when released. Then have him test the leaf by dropping it over the bull's-eye once for each category. Direct the child to record his results on the chart after each drop. Then have him glue his leaf next to his data on the chart. It's recorded—this activity scores big!

Fall, Leaves, Fall

Name	Spins ☺=yes ☹=no	Falls F=fast S=slow	Bull's-Eye ☺=yes ☹=no	Leaf
Brynn	☺	F	☺	
Zack	☹	S	☺	
Pam	☺	F	☹	

My
Leaf
Book

by _____

The Blade

1

The Veins

2

The Stem

3

The _____ Leaf

4

Pumpkin Science

Pokin' around the pumpkin patch we found lots of activities to develop youngsters' science process skills. It's time for your preschool scientists to ponder the properties of pumpkins. Let the investigations begin!

by Lucia Kemp Henry

Inferring

Undercover Pumpkin

Challenge your little ones to think like scientists with this guessing game. While students are out of the room, drape a cloth over a pumpkin so that it covers the pumpkin but still shows its size and shape. During a group time, use the riddle in the speech bubble to prompt the class to guess the identity of the hidden pumpkin. Your curious kiddies will become science sleuths quicker than you can say "jack-o'-lantern"!

Here is something you can't see. Listen to these clues to guess what it might be.
It grows from a seed, but it isn't a weed.
It has a stem. It sits on the ground. Its shape is kind of round.
Its color is orange like a tangerine. It smiles at you on Halloween.

Observing

huge

bumpy

yellow orange

Pumpkin Perceptions

Once your students have identified the seasonal subject to be studied, lead them in using their observation skills to learn more about the pumpkin. Have your group sit in a circle on the floor around the pumpkin. In turn, invite pairs of children to sit by the pumpkin so that they can touch it, smell it, and look at it closely. Encourage the children to communicate their observations by sharing words that describe the size, shape, color, and texture of the pumpkin. Record the words used to describe the pumpkin on separate cards. Later, reinforce these new science words by using them in the peppy, pumpkin-themed song that follows on page 15.

Descriptive Ditty

Your students will be pros at describing pumpkins after singing this descriptive ditty. Add new verses to the song by replacing the underlined words with the words you recorded on cards in "Pumpkin Perceptions" on page 14. Singing is a great way to communicate scientific findings!

(sung to the tune of "Pawpaw Patch")

Where, oh, where can we find pumpkins?
Where, oh, where can we find pumpkins?
Where can we find [round, round] pumpkins?
Way down yonder in the pumpkin patch!

Where, oh, where can we find pumpkins?
Where, oh, where can we find pumpkins?
Where can we find [bumpy] pumpkins?
Way down yonder in the pumpkin patch!

Making Models

Model Pumpkins

It's natural for preschool science studies to include model making, especially when models are molded from play dough! To prepare, use your favorite recipe to make a large batch of orange play dough. If desired, also prepare a batch of brown play dough for students to use to make stems. Invite each child to a center to feel the entire surface of the same pumpkin that was used for the previous activities. Then give the child a portion of the dough to shape into a miniature model of the pumpkin. Display the real pumpkin, the pumpkin models, and the word cards together on a table. Now that's a model way for your little ones to record their pumpkin observations!

Pam Crane

15

A Bunch of Pumpkins

Stimulate your little scientists' classification skills by having them study the features of a number of pumpkins in a variety of shapes, sizes, and colors. Have youngsters join you on the floor to take a close look at the pumpkins. Then ask them to help you divide them into several smaller groups so that the pumpkins in each group are similar. For example, group the pumpkins with brown bumps together. Or group pumpkins with and without stems. Record the descriptive phrase for each set on a separate index card. During a different group time, select one of the cards. Then challenge the students to classify the group of pumpkins by selecting the corresponding pumpkins on their own.

smooth

bumpy

Roll, Pumpkins, Roll!

Keep on rolling with science process skills with this activity that gets youngsters predicting. Arrange the pumpkins from "A Bunch of Pumpkins" in a line on an uncarpeted floor. To begin, roll a ball on the floor, pointing out that you were able to roll it in a straight line. Next, pick out the roundest pumpkin in the bunch and ask students to suggest how the pumpkin is similar to the ball. Ask them to predict whether the pumpkin will roll in a straight line like the ball. Have a volunteer roll the pumpkin; then discuss the results. Have students predict and then test how well each remaining pumpkin rolls. Once youngsters have identified the best rollers, discuss why some pumpkins can stick to the straight and narrow and why some pumpkins can't!

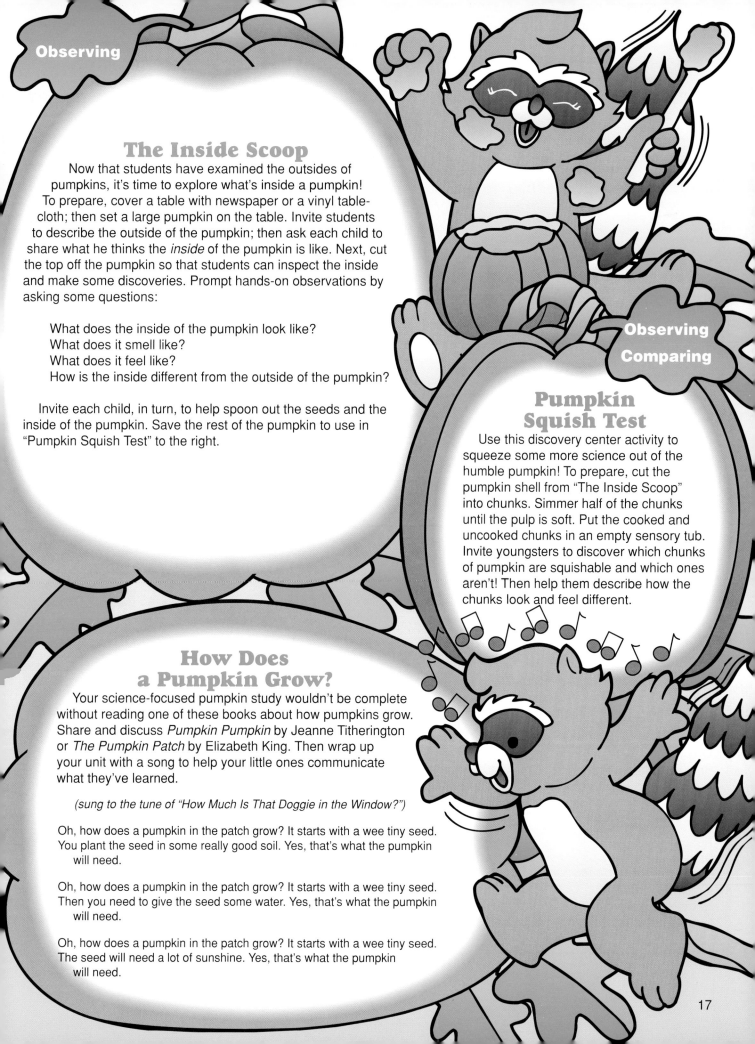

The Inside Scoop

Now that students have examined the outsides of pumpkins, it's time to explore what's inside a pumpkin! To prepare, cover a table with newspaper or a vinyl table-cloth; then set a large pumpkin on the table. Invite students to describe the outside of the pumpkin; then ask each child to share what he thinks the *inside* of the pumpkin is like. Next, cut the top off the pumpkin so that students can inspect the inside and make some discoveries. Prompt hands-on observations by asking some questions:

What does the inside of the pumpkin look like?
What does it smell like?
What does it feel like?
How is the inside different from the outside of the pumpkin?

Invite each child, in turn, to help spoon out the seeds and the inside of the pumpkin. Save the rest of the pumpkin to use in "Pumpkin Squish Test" to the right.

Pumpkin Squish Test

Use this discovery center activity to squeeze some more science out of the humble pumpkin! To prepare, cut the pumpkin shell from "The Inside Scoop" into chunks. Simmer half of the chunks until the pulp is soft. Put the cooked and uncooked chunks in an empty sensory tub. Invite youngsters to discover which chunks of pumpkin are squishable and which ones aren't! Then help them describe how the chunks look and feel different.

How Does a Pumpkin Grow?

Your science-focused pumpkin study wouldn't be complete without reading one of these books about how pumpkins grow. Share and discuss *Pumpkin Pumpkin* by Jeanne Titherington or *The Pumpkin Patch* by Elizabeth King. Then wrap up your unit with a song to help your little ones communicate what they've learned.

(sung to the tune of "How Much Is That Doggie in the Window?")

Oh, how does a pumpkin in the patch grow? It starts with a wee tiny seed.
You plant the seed in some really good soil. Yes, that's what the pumpkin
  will need.

Oh, how does a pumpkin in the patch grow? It starts with a wee tiny seed.
Then you need to give the seed some water. Yes, that's what the pumpkin
  will need.

Oh, how does a pumpkin in the patch grow? It starts with a wee tiny seed.
The seed will need a lot of sunshine. Yes, that's what the pumpkin
  will need.

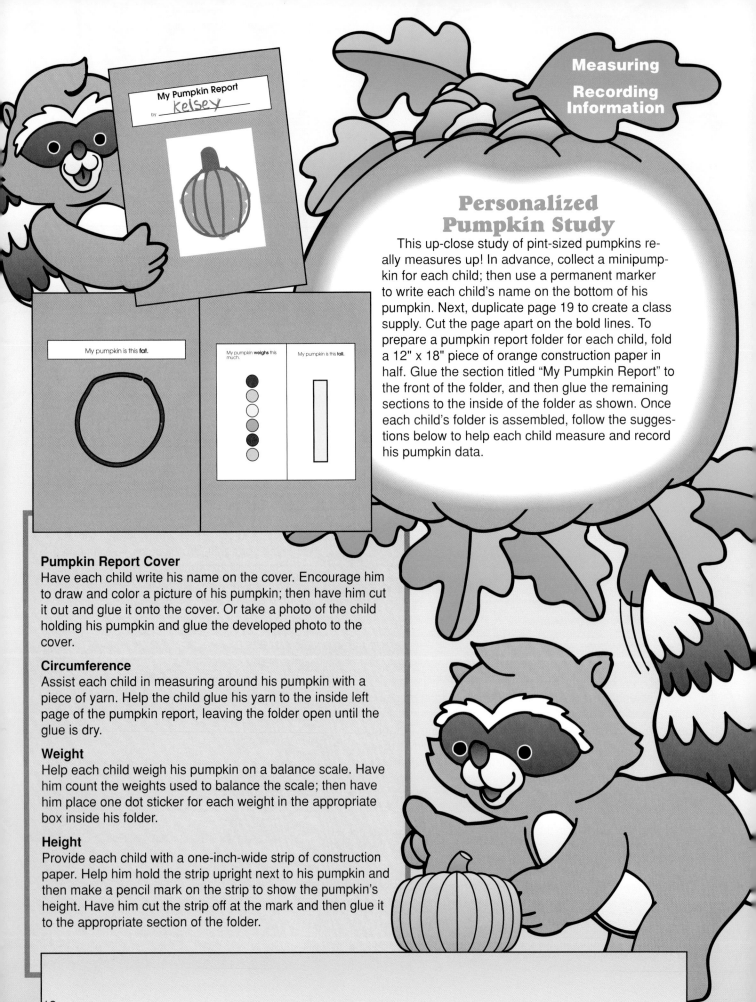

My Pumpkin Report
by Kelsey

My pumpkin is this **fat.**

My pumpkin **weighs** this much.

My pumpkin is this **tall.**

Personalized Pumpkin Study

This up-close study of pint-sized pumpkins really measures up! In advance, collect a minipumpkin for each child; then use a permanent marker to write each child's name on the bottom of his pumpkin. Next, duplicate page 19 to create a class supply. Cut the page apart on the bold lines. To prepare a pumpkin report folder for each child, fold a 12" x 18" piece of orange construction paper in half. Glue the section titled "My Pumpkin Report" to the front of the folder, and then glue the remaining sections to the inside of the folder as shown. Once each child's folder is assembled, follow the suggestions below to help each child measure and record his pumpkin data.

Pumpkin Report Cover
Have each child write his name on the cover. Encourage him to draw and color a picture of his pumpkin; then have him cut it out and glue it onto the cover. Or take a photo of the child holding his pumpkin and glue the developed photo to the cover.

Circumference
Assist each child in measuring around his pumpkin with a piece of yarn. Help the child glue his yarn to the inside left page of the pumpkin report, leaving the folder open until the glue is dry.

Weight
Help each child weigh his pumpkin on a balance scale. Have him count the weights used to balance the scale; then have him place one dot sticker for each weight in the appropriate box inside his folder.

Height
Provide each child with a one-inch-wide strip of construction paper. Help him hold the strip upright next to his pumpkin and then make a pencil mark on the strip to show the pumpkin's height. Have him cut the strip off at the mark and then glue it to the appropriate section of the folder.

My Pumpkin Report

by _____

©The Mailbox®

My pumpkin is this **fat.**

My pumpkin **weighs** this much.	My pumpkin is this **tall.**

Wonders Never Cease

Simple Science for Young Children

The "A-maize-ing" Corn Plant

Corn chips, corn dogs, cornflakes, corn bread, corn syrup—and the list goes on and on. Corn, also called *maize,* is a very important crop in the United States as well as in the world. Use the ideas in this unit to introduce your students to corn and its many, many uses.

by Ann Flagg

Objective: Students will learn that corn is a food that comes from a plant and can be used in a variety of ways.

What's That Sound? What's That Smell?

Entice youngsters into the study of corn with a guessing game. Prepare a popcorn popper; then put it behind a screen. Gather children around; then plug it in. Explain that you'd like them to discover what they are going to study by using their senses. As the popcorn begins to pop, ask "What do you hear?" and "What do you smell?" After children have identified the popcorn, they will be ready to brainstorm. Ask students what they already know about corn and write their responses on a large popcorn cutout. As you continue your study, corn ideas and corn vocabulary are sure to pop up. As they do, record them on your popcorn chart.

Corn
- It could be on a cob.
- It's salty and good.
- You have to take the leaves off.
- It pops.
- It could be corn dogs!
- My grandpa grows it.
- Corn is yellowish.
- It's good for a movie.
- It can be white.

So Where're Ya' From?

Ask children where they think popcorn comes from. After discussing ideas, show each child a kernel of unpopped popcorn. Who would think that fluffy white popcorn comes from those tiny, yellowish kernels? Explain that when a kernel is heated, steam is created inside the kernel. The pressure of the steam causes the kernel to explode and turn inside out. The result? Popcorn!

Next, establish the connection between the corn kernel and the cob by showing youngsters a cob of popcorn (available at novelty gift/kitchen shops). Pop out a kernel from the cob and have children compare it to the original kernel.

Did You Know?

Popcorn is one of the oldest kinds of corn. It was grown by Native Americans thousands of years ago!

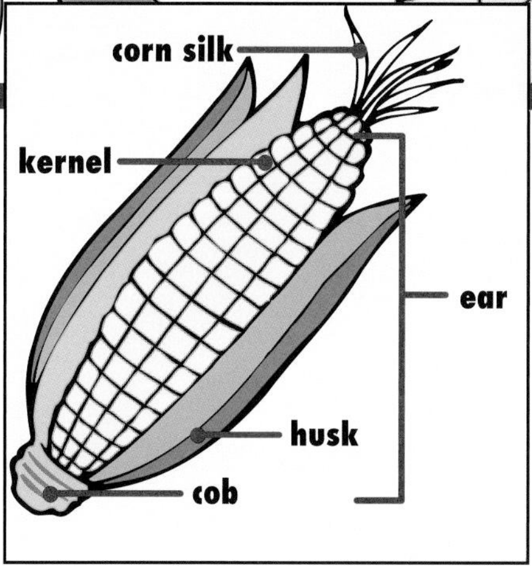

Corny Vocabulary

Hands-on exploration will help youngsters retain this new corny vocabulary. Give each child (or small group of children) an ear of Indian corn with the husk still attached. Encourage youngsters to examine their ears of corn and share what they observe. At an appropriate time in your discussion, introduce the vocabulary shown in the diagram.

(diagram labels: corn silk, kernel, ear, husk, cob)

I Say, It's a Seed!

Now that you've made the connection between popcorn and corn on the cob, help children understand that the little kernel is also a seed that can be planted to produce another corn plant. For each child, arrange a folded paper towel in a resealable plastic bag. Staple across the center of the bag to stabilize the paper towel (and the kernels). Lightly water the paper towel, leaving about one-half inch of water at the bottom of the bag. Then place corn kernels in a row above the staples. Tape each bag to a window or tack it to a bulletin board. Encourage children to observe their plants each day and to record changes that they see.

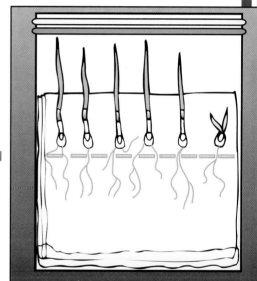

Knee High by the Fourth of July

Have your students had the opportunity to stand right next to a cornstalk? If they haven't, you can practice a little measuring to put this plant in perspective. In the Corn Belt—the midwestern states where corn is chiefly produced—cornstalks average about nine feet tall. Divide your class into small groups. Give each group a 12-inch ruler and a supply of Unifix cubes. Ask each child to put cubes together to match the length of the ruler. When each group has nine lengths of cubes (each one foot long), have students connect the lengths to make one long line. Next, have each group slide its line of cubes onto a long length of green bulletin board paper. Draw a line loosely around the cubes; then cut on the resulting outline. This will be the stalk. Mount the stalks on a classroom wall and have children use their free time to complete the scene by adding construction paper leaves and ears of corn. Encourage children to walk among your classroom cornfield comparing their heights to that of the cornstalks. Is your corn as high as an elephant's eye?

Corn, Corn Everywhere!

Corn has been called the most important crop grown in the United States—and it seems to be popping up all over! Challenge your little ones to search their homes to find corn products. Then duplicate page 23 for each child. Encourage each child to look around his home and copy the names of everything he can find that is made with corn. Then have him bring his page back to school. In turn, have each child share his list as you record each corny item. After each child has shared, count 'em up! How many did you get?

At Home With Corn

I found...
corn bread
popcorn
taco chips
cornflakes
dried corn
tortillas

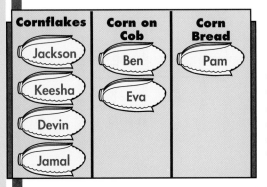

Cornflakes	Corn on Cob	Corn Bread
Jackson	Ben	Pam
Keesha	Eva	
Devin		
Jamal		

How Do You Like Your Corn?

If you made the class list described in "Corn, Corn Everywhere!", choose three (or more) of the most-mentioned entries. Then make a graph using those entries. Prepare samplings of each of the forms of corn on your graph. Before tasting, photocopy and personalize a corn pattern (below) for each child. Then have each child taste each entry. Afterward, have him tape his ear of corn on the graph to indicate which one he liked the best. How do you like your corn?

Corn Pattern

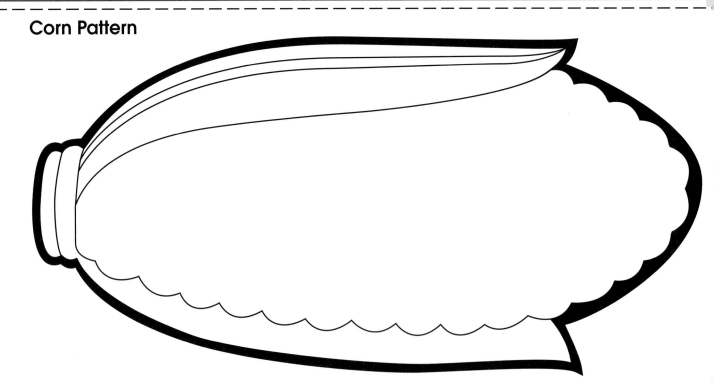

At Home With Corn

I found...

Weather Wise

"Whooo" knows about the weather? Your little ones will after you share the fun ideas and activities in this unit!

by Ada Goren

Group Time

Weather Wear

Begin your weather unit with a sorting activity that will get your students thinking about what they wear in different types of weather. To prepare, label three boxes as shown. Gather a variety of children's clothing and accessories appropriate for the three types of weather.

Set up the three boxes in your group area. Show youngsters one item at a time and ask a child to place it in the box that shows the corresponding type of weather. Talk about why the various items are worn or used in each type of weather. After the sorting is finished, place the items in your dramatic-play area for youngsters to use independently.

Storytime

Reading Up a Storm

The forecast calls for good books galore at storytime! Add to your weather theme by donning sunglasses, a rain hat, or a pair of woolly mittens as you share some of these selections!

What Can You Do in the Rain? and
What Can You Do in the Sun?
By Anna Grossnickle Hines

The Wind Blew
By Pat Hutchins

The Snowy Day
By Ezra Jack Keats

We like the sun. It's lots of fun!

We like the snow. It's cool, you know!

We like raindrops. We think they're tops!

Math Activity

Picture-Perfect Weather

Different people enjoy different types of weather. What kind of weather do *your* students like best? Find out when you create this display, which doubles as a weather-preference chart. Begin by dividing a bulletin board into three sections. Label each section with the weather icon and rhyme shown. Next, gather a pair of sunglasses, a pair of mittens and a scarf, and a child's umbrella. Ask one child at a time to tell you which of the three types of weather she likes best. Then take an instant photo of her dressed for that weather. After everyone has voted, post the photos in the appropriate sections of the bulletin board. Gather your little ones around to view the photos. As a class, count the number of children who prefer each type of weather. What's the favorite weather in your classroom?

Science Activity

Weather Wheels

Is the weather outside frightful or delightful? Your young weather watchers can make a daily report to their families with the help of these weather wheels. To prepare, duplicate page 29 to make a class supply. Have a child color the wedges on his copy as desired before cutting them out. Direct him to glue the four wedges to a white paper plate as shown. Then help him cut out the arrow and attach it to the center of the plate with a metal brad. Encourage little ones to take their weather wheels home and post them in a prominent place. Each day, a child can report on the weather he observes by pointing the arrow to the corresponding section on the wheel.

Weather Tunes

Start each day of your weather unit with a sing-along! These kid-friendly ditties cover the weather from sunny to stormy, and the motions and special effects will have your weather watchers wiggling and giggling!

Sunshine
(sung to the tune of "You Are My Sunshine")

Outside there's sunshine.	*Use arms to form circle sun overhead.*
There's lots of sunshine.	*Use arms to form circle sun overhead.*
And not a cloud in	
The sky so blue!	*Shade eyes and look upward.*
So let's go outside!	*Point thumb toward door.*
Let's not stay inside!	*Shake index finger "no."*
I'll spend my sunny days with you!	*Point to self, then others.*

Pam Crane

Do You Love the Snow?
(sung to the tune of "Do Your Ears Hang Low?")

Do you love the snow?	*Put both hands over heart.*
You can play in it, you know!	*Point to others.*
You can make a big snowball	*Use both hands to form big circle.*
Or a snowman really tall!	*Indicate "tall" with one hand.*
You can travel on your skis;	*Pretend to grip ski poles and move hips.*
Make an angel if you please!	*Wave both arms as if making snow angel.*
Do you love the snow?	*Put both hands over heart.*

26

Lightning and Thunder

Give each child a flashlight and an aluminum pie pan to use for the sight and sound effects in this song. Dim your classroom lights to get the stormy mood just right!

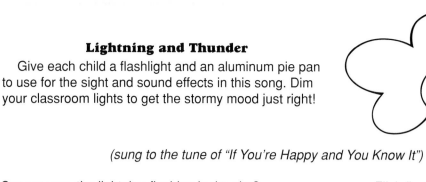

(sung to the tune of "If You're Happy and You Know It")

Can you see the lightning flashing in the sky?   *Flick flashlight on and off.*
Can you see the lightning flashing in the sky?   *Flick flashlight on and off.*
Can you see the lightning flash? Then it's followed by a crash!   *Bang hand against pie pan.*
Can you see the lightning flashing in the sky?   *Flick flashlight on and off.*

I Love Windy Weather
(sung to the tune of "I'm a Little Teapot")

I love windy weather!   *Put both hands over heart.*
See it blow.   *Shade eyes and look around.*
Watch the trees move to and fro.   *Put both arms up and sway body.*
Feel it on my face and in my hair.   *Touch hands to face, then hair.*
How I love that playful air!   *Put both hands over heart.*

27

Weather Art

Rain, clouds, snow, and sun—making all types of weather is really fun! And your youngsters can easily make this craft, which shows all four of these weather conditions. To begin, fold a sheet of white construction paper into four equal columns. Have each child follow the directions below to complete her project. When the paint and glue are dry, send these crafts home to prompt discussions about weather.

First column: Press on blue tempera paint fingerprints to make rain.

Second column: Color the space blue; then glue on bits of white paper doilies to make snow.

Third column: Sponge-paint a yellow circle sun in the center; then add rays with gold glitter glue.

Fourth column: Color the space gray; then glue on torn pieces of cotton balls for clouds.

Snack Activity

Sunny or Snowy Snacks

After crafting the project in "Weather Art," your little ones will enjoy visiting your snack table to create these edible weather pictures! Have each child choose to make either a sunny or a snowy snack. Then guide him through the preparations. Serve sunny snacks with cups of ice-cold lemonade. Serve snowy snacks with cups of warm milk. Yum!

Sunny Snack

graham cracker
blue-tinted frosting
vanilla wafer
yellow decorator icing

Frost the graham cracker with blue frosting to make the sky. Place the vanilla wafer in the center of the graham cracker. Squeeze icing from the tube to create rays for the cookie sun.

Snowy Snack

graham cracker
blue-tinted frosting
mini marshmallows

Frost the graham cracker with blue frosting to make the sky. Add mini marshmallows all over the graham cracker to resemble snowflakes.

Weather Wheel Patterns

Use with "Weather Wheels" on page 25.

sunny
The Mailbox® • Science • TEC1493
snowy
rainy
cloudy

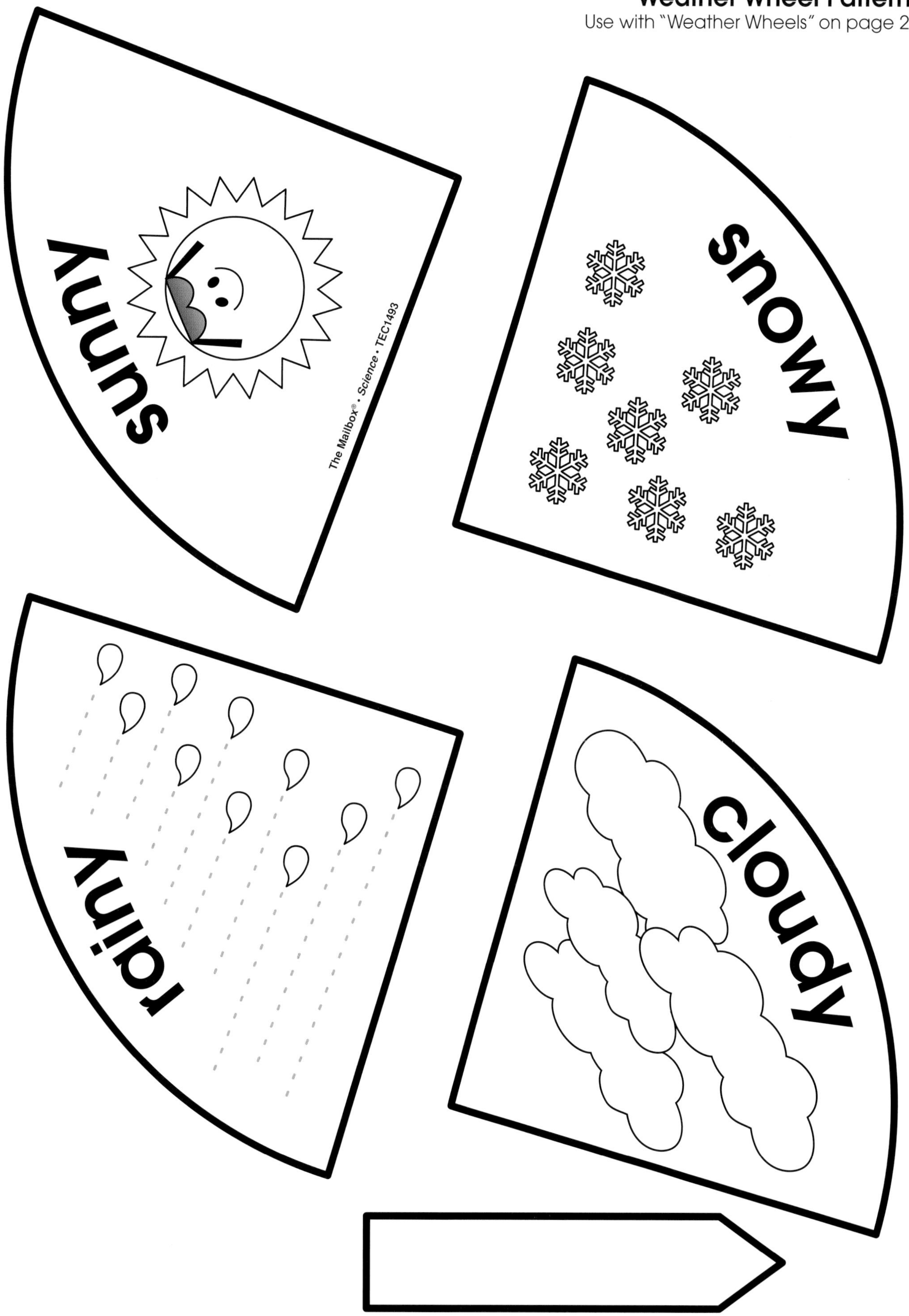

Explorations

Sun Power
Shed light on the effects of solar radiation with this simple investigation!

Provide each child with a sheet of construction paper. If desired, provide plastic magnifying lenses for each child to use as she examines her paper.

Invite each child to choose two cardboard leaf shapes.

Have each child remove the leaves from her paper and examine the prints created. Review students' predictions and then discuss the results of the investigation.

Place the sun prints and the leaf cutouts at a center. Encourage each child to visit the area and match the leaves with the prints.

Science You Can Do
by Suzanne Moore

To learn about the effects of solar radiation, you will need the following:
sunny autumn day (or 2)
2 cardboard leaf cutouts for each child
9" x 12" sheet of construction paper for each child (For best results, use thin, inexpensive construction paper.)

STEP 3

I think the paper will burn up!
Cam

I think the paper will curl.
William

I think the paper will be warm.
Joshua

Have students predict what might happen when the cardboard leaves are placed on the paper and then set in direct sunlight. Record their responses on a chart.

STEP 4

Have each child place her paper near a sunny window in direct sunlight. Then have her arrange her leaves on the paper. Leave the papers in the light for several hours.

This Is Why

- Sunlight is a form of energy called *radiation*.
- Radiation causes the paper to fade.
- The cardboard shapes block the radiation and prevent the paper beneath them from fading.

What Now?

Repeat the activity using waxed paper leaves, clear plastic wrap, and foil shapes. Which items protect the paper from radiation and create prints?

Explorations

Color Swirl
Science concepts flow naturally out of this colorful science activity.

Just prior to trying this experiment with a small group, set out a pan and jar lid for each child. Pour enough milk into each pan to cover the bottom of the pan. Pour a small amount of liquid dish detergent in each lid.

STEP 2

Help each child squeeze one drop of four different food colorings into his milk near the edge of the pan. Encourage the children to observe the drops of food coloring, being careful not to touch or move the pans. After allowing time for comments, ask some questions:

What happened when the drops of food coloring touched the milk?
Did the whole pan of milk change color?

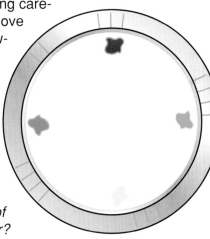

STEP 5

Direct each child to pour his milk into a sink, then use a paper towel to wipe his pan dry. Again pour milk into each child's pan. Ask students to predict what will happen if the detergent is added first and the food colorings are added second. Help each child squeeze a drop or two of the detergent in the center of the milk in his pan; then help him add a few drops of different colors of food coloring on top of the detergent. (Be sure not to stir the milk.) Discuss how the colors swirl at a slower pace.

STEP 6

Help each child recall the experiments by asking some questions:

The soap and the colors dance together in the milk.
Jason

What do you think makes the food coloring swirl in the milk?
What happened when the detergent-covered toothpick touched the food coloring?

Record each child's observations and explanations.

Science You Can Do *by Suzanne Moore*

To conduct color-swirling experiments, you will need the following:

aluminum pie pan for each child in a small group
whole milk, enough to cover the bottom of
     each child's pan twice
jar lid for each child
liquid dish detergent in a squeeze bottle
food coloring (red, blue, green, and yellow)
toothpick for each child

paper towels
chart paper
marker

STEP 3

Assist each child in squeezing a drop of liquid dish detergent into the center of the milk in his pan. Allow time for youngsters to verbalize their observations as the food coloring swirls together to create unique designs.

STEP 4

Direct each child to dip a toothpick into the jar lid of dish detergent, then into the milk. Remind him to dip the toothpick into the milk or color without stirring it. Again, invite the children to make observations as new color patterns are created. (If the swirling in a child's pan stops, add more food coloring and/or dish detergent.)

This Is Why

Milk is mostly water. The water in the milk forms an invisible skin on the surface of the milk. This skin is created by *surface tension*. When the food coloring is added to the milk, the skin supports it. But when the detergent touches the milk, the surface tension breaks, pulling the skin to the edge of the pan. This causes the colors to swirl!

What Now?

Try another experiment with milk and soap. Again pour milk into a pan. This time, shake some cinnamon on the milk. Then dip the corner of a bar of soap into the center of the milk in the pan. What happens to the cinnamon? Encourage careful observation; then discuss the results.

Same and Different... It All Makes Sense!

Your youngsters will be seeing double, tasting a difference, and tickling their five senses with these engaging activities that reinforce the concept of same and different.

ideas contributed by Michele Dare and dayle timmons

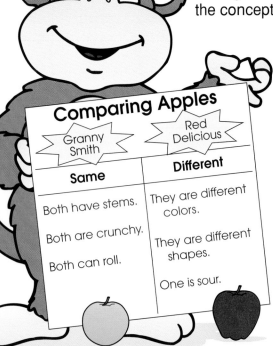

Comparing Apples

Granny Smith	Red Delicious
Same	**Different**
Both have stems.	They are different colors.
Both are crunchy.	They are different shapes.
Both can roll.	One is sour.

Taste Test

Reinforce the concept of same and different with this tasty activity. To begin, provide each child with a small paper plate and two pieces of a peeled Red Delicious apple. Invite your youngsters to munch on the apples and compare the taste. Lead students to conclude that they taste the *same.* Next, provide each child with a peeled piece of a Granny Smith apple and a peeled piece of a Red Delicious apple; then have students compare the taste of the two apples. This time students will discover that the taste is *different.* Show students a Granny Smith apple and a Red Delicious apple. Identify each one; then have your little ones examine the apples and compare other similarities and differences. Write their responses on a chart similar to the one shown. How "apple-tizing"!

Sounds Like...

Little ears will perk up with this sound-matching activity. In advance, collect a supply of opaque film canisters. (Check with your local film developer for donations.) Fill pairs of containers with matching items, such as pennies, rice, sand, or pebbles. Secure the lids with duct tape; then label the bottoms of each pair with matching stickers for self-checking. Place the canisters at a center. Invite youngsters to shake the canisters, match pairs that sound alike, and then check their work.

As a variation, fill a supply of canisters with the same item; then label the bottoms with matching stickers. Next, fill one canister with a different item and then label the bottom of that canister with a different sticker. Place all of the canisters at a center. Invite each child to shake the canisters, find the one that sounds different, and then look at the bottoms of the canisters to check his work. Sounds like fun!

Special Touches

The concept of *same* will really touch your youngsters in this sensory table idea! To prepare, fill your sensory table or a large plastic tub with rice or sand. Then hide in the sand pairs of items with distinctively different shapes or textures, such as pom-poms, counting blocks, and crayons. Cover the table or tub with a sheet. Invite each child to place her hands under the sheet and use her sense of touch to find matching items. (No peeking!) Periodically replace the items at the center to maintain student interest. Can't you just feel the excitement?

The Nose Knows

Is it the same? Is it different? The nose knows! Use this center idea to get your youngsters sniffing out spicy similarities. To prepare, gather a supply of wooden ice-cream spoons. Then hot-glue a different spice to each spoon. (For best results, use strong, distinctive spices such as ground nutmeg, garlic powder, and cloves.) Place the spoons at a center along with the spice containers. Then invite youngsters to use their sense of smell to pair each spoon with its matching container. To make the center self-checking, place a sticker on the back of each spoon; then place an identical sticker on the matching container. What fragrant learning fun!

adapted from an idea by Meg Ferguson, Birmingham, AL

A *Different* Kind of Game

Little ones will be seeing double with this exciting game that reinforces basic skills. In advance, prepare flash cards, each with pairs of matching stickers, colors, shapes, letters, or numbers. Then create two or three more cards, each with two different stickers, shapes, letters, or numbers. Place all of the cards in one pile. Then have a small group of students arrange chairs in a semicircle. Have each child sit in a chair; then show your youngsters a flash card. If the two items on the card match, direct your little ones to say, "Same!" and remain seated. If the items on the card do not match, instruct your little ones to say, "Different!" and then quickly move to a different chair within the semicircle. Continue playing until all of the flash cards have been revealed. Your students will be up and learning with this idea!

Wanted: Germ Fighters

Germs should beware! Begin the year with these activities and your youngsters will become germ fighters all year!

Cover Your Mouth and Nose

This simple demonstration will help your students understand how sneezes and coughs spread germs. To prepare, draw a face on a paper plate and then cut holes where the mouth and nose are located. Fill a spray bottle with water. Hold the plate up to your face. As you pretend to sneeze, spray water through the openings from the back of the plate to simulate germs exiting a person's mouth and nose. Repeat the sneeze, but this time have a child hold a tissue over the mouth and nose area. Discuss the differences between the two sneezes and the importance of covering our mouths and noses when we cough or sneeze. Achoo!

Judy Pilcher
Moscow, ID

Glitter Germs

Germs aren't only spread through the air but also by touch. To demonstrate this, have your students sit in a circle; then apply a liberal amount of lotion that contains glitter to your hand. Explain to students that the glitter in the lotion represents germs. Shake a student's hand; then have him use the same hand to shake his neighbor's hand. Instruct students to continue shaking hands around the circle in the same manner. After each handshake, have each student look at his hand to see if any germs were passed to him. Discuss with youngsters how germs were passed from person to person and the importance of keeping our hands clean. Then take a trip to the sink to wash away all the germs from this activity!

Cristin Cates—Grs. K–1
Fort Gordon School-Age Services
Fort Gordon, GA

DID YOU KNOW?
Bacteria and viruses are tiny living things commonly called germs. As many as 100 million bacteria may be contained in one grain of soil!

Stop Germs

Your germ busters will learn ways to stop germs with this activity. In advance, cut a large octagon from red poster board and then glue it to the center of a sheet of white poster board. Write "STOP GERMS" in the center of the octagon. Make mini signs by cutting a small red construction paper octagon for each child. Program each one with the phrase "Ask me how to STOP germs!"

Discuss with students where germs can be found and how they can be spread. Then have youngsters brainstorm a list of ways in which we can stop the spread of germs, such as keeping clean, using bandages, or brushing teeth. Write students' responses around the octagon; then review the list. After the lesson, tape a mini sign to each child's shirt and encourage her to share the information she's learned about stopping germs!

adapted from an idea by Judy Pilcher

Keep your hands clean.
STOP GERMS
Use bandages.
Brush your teeth.

Read aloud *Germs! Germs! Germs!* by Bobbi Katz.

Winter Science

Winter Where You Are

Whether your winter is cold and snowy, wet and rainy, or warm and sunny, these cross-curricular ideas and activities will create the perfect learning climate in your classroom.

ideas contributed by Lucia Kemp Henry

It's Winter!
What's Our Weather Like?

Thunderstorms or snowstorms? How about brainstorms? This circle-time activity has youngsters brainstorming words that describe winter in your neck of the woods. To begin, have your students close their eyes and imagine a typical winter day. Invite each child to share a descriptive weather word; then write his response on a sheet of chart paper. Review the completed chart with students before displaying it in your classroom. Refer to the chart again in "Sing a Weather Song" (below).

Our winter is...

rainy	gloomy
cloudy	chilly
cool	damp
wet	muddy
dark	stormy

Sing a Weather Song

Once students are familiar with your list of weather words (see "It's Winter! What's Our Weather Like?"), have them sing the song at the right, replacing the underlined words with words from the chart. If needed, replace the italicized phrase with another phrase that more accurately describes your winter weather—such as *raindrops pouring* or *sunlight shining.*

(sung to the tune of
"If You're Happy and You Know It")

When it's winter in our town, it is [cold].
When it's winter in our town, it is [cold].
When it's winter in our town, we see
snowflakes falling down.
When it's winter in our town, it is [cold].

Winter Wear for Winter Where?

Would you wear mittens during winter in San Diego? How about shorts on a typical Detroit winter day? Help your little ones sort out winter weather differences with this group flannelboard activity. In advance, obtain pictures of different types of climates, such as rainy, sunny, snowy, and mild. (Calendars are a good source.) Laminate the pictures and then glue a strip of felt to the back of each one. Next, duplicate the clothing patterns on pages 41 and 42. Color, cut out, and laminate the clothing; then glue a strip of felt to the back of each piece. Place the pictures and clothing on a flannelboard; then invite students to match the clothes with the appropriate climate. Discuss the differences in clothing for each climate; then have students determine which set is most like the clothing needed for winter weather in your area.

Wonderful Winter Wear!

Now that your youngsters have warmed up to the idea of different winter climates, heat up their reading skills with these individual booklets. To prepare, copy for each child pages 43–45 and the clothing patterns from pages 41 and 42 that are most appropriate for winter in your area. (Do not use the hats.) Cut apart the booklet pages; then provide each child with a set of pages and a page of clothing patterns. Have the child follow the directions below to complete his booklet. When the glue is dry, stack the pages in order, and then staple them together along the left side.

Cover: Write your name where indicated; then embellish as desired with various craft items.
Page 1: Color the page; then glue sand to the bottom of the page.
Page 2: Draw raindrops on the page. Squeeze yellow glue on the raincoat and boots; then use your finger to spread the glue over the coat and boots. Cut an umbrella canopy from fabric (see sample) and glue it to the umbrella handle.
Page 3: Color the page; glue cotton ball pieces to the coat and the bottom of the page to resemble snow.
Page 4: Color and cut out the clothing patterns. Glue them onto the figure and then color the head to look like yourself.

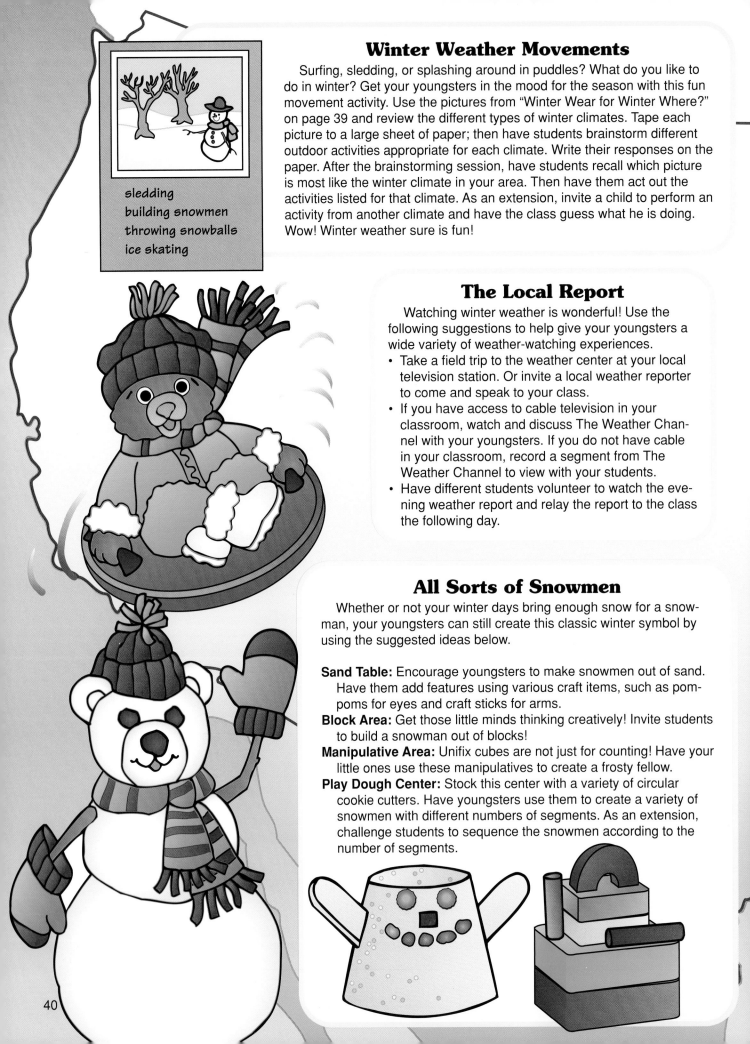

sledding
building snowmen
throwing snowballs
ice skating

Winter Weather Movements

Surfing, sledding, or splashing around in puddles? What do you like to do in winter? Get your youngsters in the mood for the season with this fun movement activity. Use the pictures from "Winter Wear for Winter Where?" on page 39 and review the different types of winter climates. Tape each picture to a large sheet of paper; then have students brainstorm different outdoor activities appropriate for each climate. Write their responses on the paper. After the brainstorming session, have students recall which picture is most like the winter climate in your area. Then have them act out the activities listed for that climate. As an extension, invite a child to perform an activity from another climate and have the class guess what he is doing. Wow! Winter weather sure is fun!

The Local Report

Watching winter weather is wonderful! Use the following suggestions to help give your youngsters a wide variety of weather-watching experiences.
- Take a field trip to the weather center at your local television station. Or invite a local weather reporter to come and speak to your class.
- If you have access to cable television in your classroom, watch and discuss The Weather Channel with your youngsters. If you do not have cable in your classroom, record a segment from The Weather Channel to view with your students.
- Have different students volunteer to watch the evening weather report and relay the report to the class the following day.

All Sorts of Snowmen

Whether or not your winter days bring enough snow for a snowman, your youngsters can still create this classic winter symbol by using the suggested ideas below.

Sand Table: Encourage youngsters to make snowmen out of sand. Have them add features using various craft items, such as pompoms for eyes and craft sticks for arms.
Block Area: Get those little minds thinking creatively! Invite students to build a snowman out of blocks!
Manipulative Area: Unifix cubes are not just for counting! Have your little ones use these manipulatives to create a frosty fellow.
Play Dough Center: Stock this center with a variety of circular cookie cutters. Have youngsters use them to create a variety of snowmen with different numbers of segments. As an extension, challenge students to sequence the snowmen according to the number of segments.

Clothing Patterns
Use with "Winter Wear for Winter Where?" and "Wonderful Winter Wear!" on page 39.

Wonderful Winter Wear!

by _____

If winter in my town was hot,

I would wear my shorts a lot.

I

Booklet Pages 2 and 3
Use with "Wonderful Winter Wear!" on page 39.

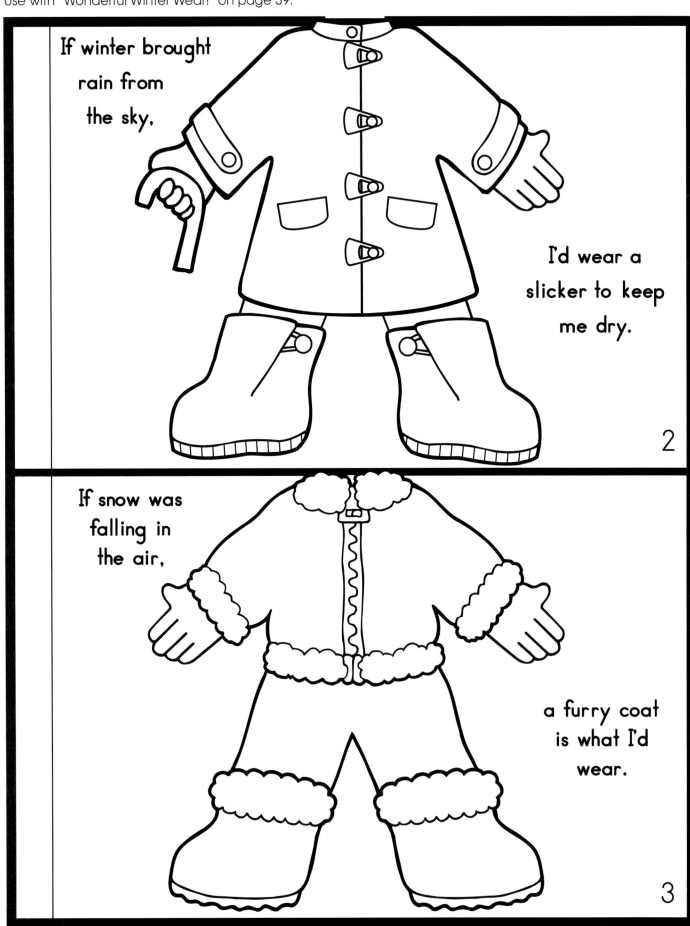

If winter brought rain from the sky,

I'd wear a slicker to keep me dry.

2

If snow was falling in the air,

a furry coat is what I'd wear.

3

Winter there.
Winter here.

This is my own
winter gear.

4

Wonders Never Cease

Simple Science for Young Children

Ice Is Nice!

Introduce your little ones to the wonderful wonders of ice! There are lots of skills that you can slip in and slide over as youngsters explore this chilly solid. So grab some ice and let's get started!

ideas by Darcy Brown and Diane Gilliam

Objective: Students will use scientific process skills to explore ice. Students will also learn that ice is a solid form of water and possesses various observable attributes.

Safety: Ice may cause numbness or tissue damage when touched for prolonged periods of time. When necessary, provide your youngsters with paper towels to cover the ice cubes before they handle them.

Predicting
Observing
Communicating

What Is Ice?

Get your little ones ready for ice exploration with this prediction activity. Show youngsters a pitcher of water. Have them tell you what is in the pitcher. Explain that water is a *liquid*—it has no shape of its own, but it does take up space. Tell youngsters that you are going to put the water in a freezer. Have youngsters predict what will happen to the water. List their predictions on chart paper. Then fill several ice trays with water, making sure each child has an ice cube. Put the trays in the cafeteria's freezer. Allow the water to freeze and then bring the trays back to the classroom. What happened to the water? Have youngsters revisit their prediction chart and circle the predictions that are correct.

What will happen to the water?
disappear—Saleen
spill out—Chris/Tanner
drip—Alexis/Joy/Ian
get cold—Marti/Becca
freeze—Jill/Timmy
get hard—Carson/Kyle
make ice—Cassidy/Corey/Allie

Ice is...
hard
quiet
clear
crunchy
melts
wet
cold
solid
slippery

Defining
Describing
Observing

Sensing Ice

Put the chill on students' vocabulary as they experience ice with all five senses. To prepare, draw a large glass of ice water with cubes similar to the one shown. Give each child an ice cube (from "What Is Ice?") and a paper towel. Encourage her to hold the ice in her hand and focus on all the ways she can describe it. Guide her to use her senses of sight, hearing, touch, smell, and taste to explore the ice. As students name descriptive words and phrases, list them on the drawn ice cubes in the glass. Then finish the display by covering each ice cube with transparency film to give the ice that *shiny, wet, clear, smooth* look!

We see ice...	We use ice...
–on mountains	–to cool food
–in glasses	–to keep drinks cold
–on lakes	–to skate on
–in the freezer	–to play hockey
–in a cooler	–on injuries
–in a snow cone	–to make ice cream
–in icebergs	–for headaches
–in the grocery store	–to live in

Classifying
Critical thinking
Communicating

I Spy

Now that your youngsters know what ice is, go a step further with this brainstorming activity. Label two sheets of chart paper as shown. Then have youngsters begin to list both where they have seen ice and the different uses for ice. Follow up the thinking by reading or paraphrasing a nonfiction book about ice, such as *Snow and Ice* (Living With the Weather Series) by Philip Steele. Encourage youngsters to add to their lists any information learned from the book.

Did You Know?
If all the earth's land ice melted, sea levels would rise about 70 meters (76.6 yards).

Critical thinking
Defining
Observing
Measuring

Expanding Ice, Expanding Minds

When water freezes, it *expands,* or takes up more space. Demonstrate this concept to your youngsters by filling a glass with ice cubes. Ask students if the glass is full. Then set it aside while the ice cubes melt. After the ice melts, have students look at the water level. Is the glass still full? What happened? Ice expands when it freezes and takes up more space. The opposite is also true—when ice melts, it takes up less space. Therefore, there is more room in the glass now that the ice has melted.

Did You Know?
Most substances contract as they freeze, but water contracts only until its temperature hits 39°F. The molecules of unfrozen water are close together and move quickly. As the water freezes, the molecules spread apart, move more slowly, and form patterns.

Explorations

C-c-cold? Put On a Jacket!

Cooler temperatures are here. To demonstrate how jackets keep body heat in and cool air out, just try these activities on for size!

STEP 1

To prepare to demonstrate how jackets keep us warm, make a hand jacket by inserting the batting pieces into one of the plastic bags.

STEP 2

Just prior to your group time, half-fill the bowls with water and ice.

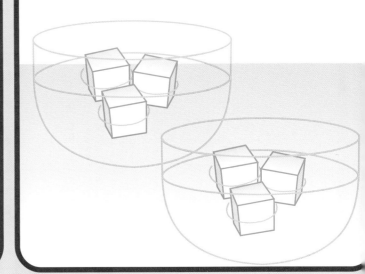

STEP 5

Have the children take off their jackets and examine them carefully. How do jackets help us stay warm?

STEP 6

Give each child an opportunity to participate in this demonstration. Have a child put one hand in the empty plastic bag and the other hand between the layers of batting in the hand jacket. Next, have him immerse each hand into one of the bowls of water.

How do his hands feel different? How is the batting in the bag like a jacket?

Science You Can Do
by Ann Flagg

To learn how jackets keep us warm, you will need the following:
a cool or cold day
children's coats
2 quart-size (7" x 8") resealable plastic bags
two 6" x 7" pieces of polyester bonded batting
2 deep bowls
ice
water

STEP 3

Ask a small group of children to gather their coats and join you in your group area. Have the children put on their coats.

Ask some questions to get youngsters warmed up for your demonstration.
- Why don't we wear jackets in the summer?
- Why do we wear jackets in the fall and winter?
- Are you comfortable wearing your coat inside the classroom?

STEP 4

Next, direct each child to feel his face with one hand and a window with the other hand. How do they feel different? Lead children to conclude that their bodies are warm and the outside air is cool.

Did You Know?

- Heat is a form of energy.
- Our bodies use the food we eat to produce the heat we need to keep our bodies at about 98.6 degrees.
- Heat flows from a warm object or area to a cooler object or area.
- Insulation stops the movement of heat.
- In cold weather we wear insulated clothing to keep body heat from escaping.
- In warm weather we wear light clothing to let heat escape from the body.
- In addition to jackets, thermos bottles and coolers are examples of insulated items that keep heat from escaping an area.

What Now?

- Animals wear coats too! Provide children with precut animal shapes, cotton balls, felt scraps, scissors, and glue. As the children glue coats onto the animals, help them understand that an animal's fur is similar to a person's coat.
- Gather clothing of varying thicknesses such as a T-shirt, a thinly lined coat, and a heavy winter coat. Have children compare the different thicknesses of the fabrics and the insulating liners.

Explorations

Brrr! It's Frosty!

Jack Frost isn't telling all of his secrets, but he is willing to share one way to make frost so that your little ones can chill out with science.

JACK

STEP 1

Ask your little ones whether they have heard of Jack Frost or seen his icy work on cold days. Next, explain that you have found out one of Jack's secrets for making frost. To begin the activity, give each child in a small group a can to fill with crushed ice. Ask the students to observe how the outsides of their cans feel.

STEP 2

Help each child measure one cup of water to pour over the crushed ice. Ask the children to watch the outsides of their cans for several minutes.

ONE CUP

STEP 5

Once a thin layer of frost forms on the outside of each child's can, ask youngsters what they think Jack's secret is. How was the frost made? Record their ideas.

I think the salt is his secret! My can has ice!

STEP 6

Use the information in "This Is Why" to explain how Jack Frost's secret ingredient (salt) made the water on the outsides of the cans turn to frost. Then sing this song to the tune of "Mr. Sun" to wrap up your chilly lesson.

Mister Frost, Frost, Mister Jack Frost,
Oh, we know your secret now.
Mister Frost, Frost, Mister Jack Frost,
Oh, we know your secret now.
Salt makes water very, very cold,
So cold it turns to ice. That is what we're told.
Mister Frost, Frost, Mister Jack Frost,
Oh, we know your secret now.

JACK

Science You Can Do
by Suzanne Moore

To make frost, you will need the following:
empty 16 oz. can for each child in a small group
   (cover the cans' rims with tape for safety)
crushed ice (enough to fill each child's can)
1 c. of water for each child
1 c. measuring cup
3 tbsp. of salt for each child
tablespoon
plastic spoon for each child

STEP 3

When water forms on the outsides of the cans, ask some questions: What did the water do to the crushed ice? How does the outside of the can feel now? What do you think makes the water on the outside of your can? Record each child's ideas.

The can shows it's cold by having water on its outside!

STEP 4

Tell your children that you have Jack Frost's secret ingredient for making frost. Then help each child add three tablespoons of salt to her can. Have her gently stir the salt into the ice water. Wait about five minutes.

This Is Why

So what is Jack Frost's secret? When the salt is added to the ice water, it makes the water inside the can colder. When the water gets colder, the can gets colder. The water on the outside of the can freezes, covering the can with frost.

What Now?

Here's another one of Jack's secrets for making frost. Slather some petroleum jelly on a glass pan. Invite several youngsters to use their fingers to make squiggly designs on the jelly. Place the pan in the freezer for two hours. When the pan is removed from the freezer, youngsters will find that a frosty coating has formed on their drawings.

Pam Crane

A GINGERBREAD "SENSE-SATION"

These activities add a touch of gingerbread and a flavor of fun to stir up some five-senses learning experiences for your youngsters.

ideas contributed by Kathy Curnow

AN INVITATION TEMPTATION

Stimulate the curiosity and senses of your little ones with this eye-appealing, sense-tickling door display. To make it, tape a length of brown bulletin board paper along your classroom door frame. Trim the paper above the door to resemble a roof. Edge the house with scalloped bulletin board trim; then paint details on the house. Next, give each child a construction paper circle and have him glue a photo of himself to the center of it. Then encourage him to decorate his cutout in lollipop style. To add fragrance to his lollipop, have him squeeze a line of glue along the edge of his circle, then sprinkle on ground cinnamon, cloves, or a flavored gelatin mix. After the glue dries, tape the end of a wide craft stick to the cutout. Attach the completed lollipops to the gingerbread-house display to make an inviting grand entry into the "scent-sational" world of gingerbread.

GINGERBREAD LISTENING

Highlight each child's sense of hearing by presenting a hearing-oriented storytime. Read aloud Paul Galdone's *The Gingerbread Boy,* but do not show the pictures. Encourage each child to close his eyes and use his sense of hearing to imagine what is happening in the story. Afterward, ask children questions about the story. As youngsters respond to your questions, ask how they knew the answers, even though they couldn't see the pictures! Guide youngsters to conclude that they could follow the story because they used the sense of hearing.

YOO-HOO! WHERE ARE YOU?

After reading the story without pictures (see "Gingerbread Listening"), invite students to participate in this game requiring sharp listening skills. In advance, make one copy of the gingerbread boy pattern (page 55) on construction paper. Cut out the pattern; then decorate it as desired. Attach a craft stick to create a stick puppet. Seat students in a circle. Designate one child to be It and to sit in the middle of the circle with her eyes closed. Then play some music and have the other students pass the puppet from child to child. Stop the music and have the child with the puppet hold it. Then instruct It, with her eyes closed, to say, "Yoo-hoo! Where are you?" Ask the child with the puppet to respond, "Here I am!" It uses her sense of hearing to identify who has the gingerbread boy. After the child is identified, she exchanges places with It. Continue in the same manner, giving each child an opportunity to be It.

GINGERBREAD VIEWERS

And now for the sense of sight! Review *The Gingerbread Boy* (see "Gingerbread Listening") with your students. Ask questions that students might only know for sure by using their sense of sight. (For example, you might ask, "What color are the Gingerbread Boy's shoes?") When you begin to get varying answers or questions, invite your youngsters to use their sense of sight as you reread the story and show the illustrations. Then ask the same questions that you asked at the beginning of this activity. Emphasize how each child's sense of sight provided him with more information.

TOUCH AND TELL

Youngsters may be quite interested to learn that hearing and seeing are not the only senses that provide us with information—the sense of touch can provide lots of information too. Invite students to play a tactile matching game. Use the pattern on page 55 to make several pairs of tagboard gingerbread boys. Apply a different texture to each pair of cutouts. For example, to one pair, glue on sandpaper. To another pair, glue on stretched-out cotton balls. To a third pair, glue on felt. To a fourth pair, glue on identical fabrics. When each set is dry, invite students to play a touch-and-tell matching game. To play, have a child close his eyes; then give him a gingerbread boy. Place its match and an additional gingerbread boy in front of the child. Encourage him to carefully feel the gingerbread boy he is holding and then feel the others to find its match. After he identifies the matching gingerbread boy, have him open his eyes and use his sense of sight to check his choice. A lot can be learned through touch alone!

THE NOSE KNOWS

Out of sight? Out of earshot? Out of touch? Then stimulate those sniffers and try smelling it out! In advance, prepare two different flavors of Jell-O Jigglers gelatin according to the package directions. Also follow the provided recipe to prepare a stiff batch of cinnamon-flavored gelatin. After each flavor of gelatin has set, cut out small gingerbread boy shapes using cookie cutters. Put a spoonful of cinnamon in a paper cup. Then place a gelatin gingerbread boy of each flavor on separate paper plates. Cover each plate with a paper towel. First, have a volunteer smell the cinnamon in the cup; then ask him to smell the gelatin on each plate (without looking) to determine which one matches the aroma of the cinnamon. When he discovers the match, ask him to use his sense of sight to check his selection. Afterward, invite him to eat one of the Jigglers shapes. Then replace the selected gelatin with one of the same flavor and repeat the exercise, giving each child an opportunity to sniff and match.

Cinnamon Gelatin

2 envelopes unflavored gelatin ½ tbsp. cinnamon 3 tbsp. sugar ½ c. cold water 1½ c. boiling water	In a large bowl, sprinkle the cold water over the gelatin. Let the mix stand for one minute; then stir in the cinnamon and sugar. Add the boiling water and stir the ingredients together until the gelatin and sugar dissolve (the cinnamon will remain grainy). Chill the gelatin until firm.

FRAGRANT FRAMES

Invite students to make a gingerbread delight that's pleasing to the sight—a scented picture frame! And, as a bonus, youngsters will use most of their other senses while making these frames. To make the dough for one frame, have a child mix four tablespoons of flour, one tablespoon of salt, two tablespoons of water, and a pinch of cinnamon or ginger spice in a bowl. Have the child knead the ingredients to form a dough. Then ask her to press out her dough and cut it with a gingerbread boy cookie cutter. Using the lid from a two-liter bottle, cut a hole in the middle of each dough cutout. Place the cutouts on a cookie sheet and bake them at 350°F for approximately 45 minutes. Then have each child paint her cooled gingerbread boy frame with tempera paint. After the paint dries, invite her to use a fine-tip permanent marker to draw on other features—such as a nose, mouth, eyes, and buttons. Spray the completed frame with clear varnish. If desired, hot-glue a decorative bow to the front of the frame and a looped ribbon to the back to create a hanger. Position and glue a photo of the child behind the frame so that the child's face can be seen through the hole. Encourage youngsters to take their framed pictures home to give as gifts or to use as holiday ornaments.

Debbie Newsome—Gr. K
Dolvin Elementary
Alpharetta, GA

ACTIVATE ALL SENSES

With all these gingerbread activities, your youngsters will be primed for a total sensory experience resulting in a treat they can sink their teeth into—gingerbread cookies! In advance, make a chart with a column labeled for each of the five senses. With the help of students, prepare gingerbread cookies following the provided recipe. As you do, ask children to comment on the many things they see, hear, feel, smell, and taste. Record youngsters' comments on the chart. Students are sure to be motivated when their senses are activated.

touch	taste	sight	hearing	smell
• cold • gooshy • soft	• yummy	• kind of tan	• smush	• Mmm! like coffee

GINGERBREAD COOKIES

(makes approximately 30 cookies)

1 c. sugar	2 tsp. baking soda
¾ c. shortening	¼ tsp. salt
1 egg	1 tsp. cinnamon
¼ cup molasses	¾ tsp. cloves
2 c. plain flour, sifted	¾ tsp. ginger

Preheat the oven to 375°F. Combine and mix the first four ingredients in a large bowl. Add the remaining ingredients and mix well to form a dough. Roll the dough onto a sheet of waxed paper. Cut the dough with gingerbread man cookie cutters; then place the cookies two inches apart on a greased cookie sheet. Bake the cookies 10–12 minutes. After the cookies cool, have each child use tube icing to decorate a cookie as desired. Then invite him to enjoy the sweet sensation of eating his cookie.

BOOKS THAT MAKE SENSE

The Listening Walk
Written by Paul Showers
Illustrated by Aliki

My Five Senses
Written and Illustrated by Aliki

Gingerbread Boy Pattern
Use with "Yoo-Hoo! Where Are You?" on page 52
and "Touch and Tell" on page 53.

MUCH ADO ABOUT
Reindeer

This time of year, fanciful flying reindeer seem to be everywhere you look—in shop windows, in advertisements, on gift wrap, and on bulletin boards. As reindeer artwork shows up in more and more places, children's imaginative musings about reindeer are bound to soar. Use the information and ideas in this unit to bring your students' thoughts about reindeer back down to earth. They may be surprised to find that real reindeer (and their caribou cousins) are as intriguing and awe inspiring as the fabled ones!

ideas contributed by Joe Appleton and Karen Shelton

REALLY? ARE REINDEER LIKE THAT?

No reindeer in sight? No problem. Use this booklet and the suggestions on page 57 to help children learn some of the characteristics of these deer. For each child, duplicate the booklet pages on pages 59–61 and cut apart the triangular pages. As you introduce each page, discuss it by sharing the corresponding information on page 57. Bring the information to life by sharing illustrations from books and completing the "Try This" activities. Then have each child color his page, drawing in more details if he wishes to. When each page has been discussed and completed, assist students in making booklet covers as described in "Simply Irresistible Booklet Covers."

Fur keeps them warm.

SIMPLY IRRESISTIBLE BOOKLET COVERS

These student-made covers can be used with "Really? Are Reindeer Like That?" to make reindeer booklets or with blank paper to make journals or other seasonal booklets. To make a cover, begin by folding an eight-inch square of construction paper to create a triangular shape. Sequence the triangular booklet pages, tuck them into the folded paper, and staple them near the fold. Glue on eyes and a nose cut from construction paper scraps. To make antlers, trace a partner's hands onto construction paper. Then cut out the hands, and glue them to the back of the booklet for antlers. There you have it! One fine reindeer booklet.

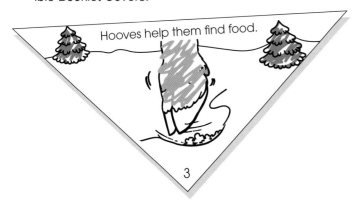
Hooves help them find food.
3

Caribou and reindeer are from the same part of the deer family, *Rangifer tarandus*. This unit focuses on the characteristics they have in common.

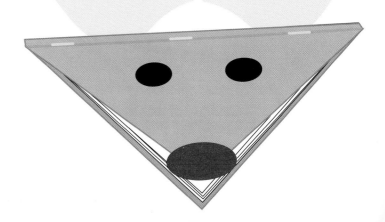

Did You Know?

Use these facts with "Really? Are Reindeer Like That?" on page 56.

All reindeer grow antlers.

BOOKLET PAGE 1—Usually only male deer have antlers. But both male and female reindeer have antlers. Reindeer have their antlers for several months; then they fall off. New ones grow back later.

TRY THIS:
Antlers can be very heavy! Have students take turns carrying a heavy book or two on their heads (using their hands to balance the books). After a few minutes, find out what this experience tells your children about reindeer.

Fur keeps them warm.

BOOKLET PAGE 2—Reindeer live where it is cold and snowy. They have special fur that keeps them warm. Next to their skin, reindeer have thick, woolly fur. During the summer, the fur thins out so the reindeer will be cooler.

TRY THIS:
Have students take turns wrapping up in several layers of warm, woolly blankets for a few minutes. If a student becomes too warm, ask him to remove only one blanket at a time. How does it feel after a blanket comes off? Can he imagine wearing woolly blankets all the time?

Hooves help them find food.

BOOKLET PAGE 3—Reindeer have hooves that spread out when they walk on them. They use their hooves like scoops when it's time to find something to eat beneath the snow.

TRY THIS:
Hide a few plastic plants beneath foam packing pieces in your sand table. Have students take turns using U-shaped plastic scoops to uncover the plants. Hey! This is what reindeer do when they are looking for plants in the snow!

Reindeer go to look for food together.

BOOKLET PAGE 4—Reindeer go from place to place looking for food to eat. They travel—or migrate—in large herds.

TRY THIS:
On the playground or in a gym, play follow-the-leader. Have children take turns leading the herd. Reindeer travel together the same way.

Reindeer live near the North Pole.

BOOKLET PAGE 5—Reindeer live near the North Pole.

TRY THIS:
Using a classroom globe, help children find the North Pole. Help them find Greenland, Alaska, Canada, Norway, and Sweden, explaining that this is where reindeer live.

Some reindeer help people.

BOOKLET PAGE 6—Some people follow reindeer herds. They make cheese and butter from reindeer milk! Other people have reindeer pull sleds and sleighs.

TRY THIS:
Attach a rope to a cardboard box (to serve as a harness as children role-play reindeer). Have children take turns loading the box with a few blocks from the block corner. Encourage children to take turns pretending to be reindeer slowly pulling the box from place to place.

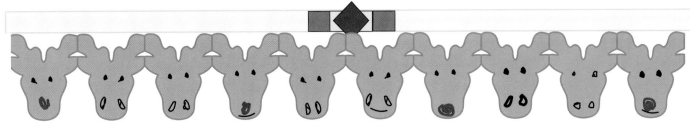

TOO MANY TO COUNT?

When they're migrating, reindeer pour over the mountains and into the valleys by the thousands. To represent an ever-growing influx of reindeer in your classroom, you'll need several 8" x 60" strips of brown bulletin board paper. Accordion-fold each strip at six-inch intervals. Enlarge the reindeer outline on page 59 so that it's about 8" x 6"; then cut it out. Trace it onto each stack of folded paper; then cut out the design, cutting through all thicknesses. (Do not cut along the dotted lines!) When each strip is unfolded, you'll have a set of ten reindeer.

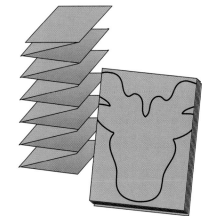

Post the first set of ten reindeer, and ask for several volunteers to color eyes and noses on the deer. Have students count the deer and post the total number nearby. The following day, repeat the process with an additional set of deer. Use all 20 reindeer for more counting practice and have students compare the totals from each day. Continue adding to your herd until all strips are used.

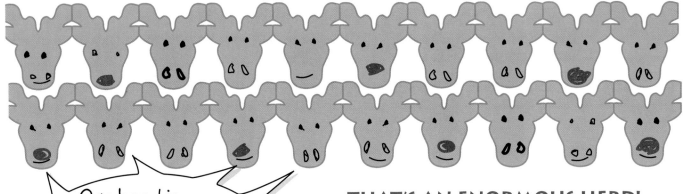

Our herd is ...
large   huge   enormous
big   giant
gargantuan   tremendous

THAT'S AN ENORMOUS HERD!

As your classroom is filling with the reindeer described in "Too Many to Count?", talk about how big—how extremely big—your herd is getting. Ask children to think of or find words that have a meaning similar to that of big. As the children contribute words over several days, post them near the reindeer. Periodically reread the words, discussing with the children which words seem to indicate the largest herd.

CLICKING ALONG

During their long, long annual migration, reindeer and caribou move in a wide range of ways. Sometimes they lope, trot, or run along. Sometimes they wheel around to escape a predator. At other times they make their way gingerly down hillsides or stroke strongly against the currents of mountain streams. Ask your students to imagine that they are reindeer and to act out several kinds of movements. After a while, explain that reindeer's hooves click as they walk, and encourage students to snap their fingers or tap rhythm sticks as they move along.

To get your children really prancing and pawing like reindeer, play recordings of several classical instrumentals. As the music plays, ask students to move to the beat as reindeer would.

Reindeer Pattern
Use with "Too Many to Count?" on page 58.

Booklet Pages 1 and 2
Use with "Really? Are Reindeer Like That?" on page 56.

All reindeer grow antlers.

Fur keeps them warm.

Bookmark

Let's read about reindeer!

Try

A Caribou Alphabet
by Mary Beth Owens

and

The Wild Christmas Reindeer
by Jan Brett

©The Mailbox®

Booklet Pages 3 and 4
Use with "Really? Are Reindeer Like That?" on page 56.

3

Hooves help them find food.

Reindeer go to look for food together.

4

Let's read about reindeer!

Try

The Wild Christmas Reindeer by Jan Brett

and

A Caribou Alphabet by Mary Beth Owens

©The Mailbox®

Booklet Pages 5 and 6
Use with "Really? Are Reindeer Like That?" on page 56.

5

Reindeer live near the North Pole.

Some reindeer help people.

©The Mailbox®

6

The Long and Short of Shadows

With groundhogs popping in and out of February shadows, what better time to embark on a study of shadows? Use the ideas in this unit to help your little ones explore the long and short of shadows.

ideas by Ann Flagg

Objective:
Students will learn that it takes light and an object to make a shadow.

Look Around You

Begin your shadow study with a look around you! Take your students outside on a sunny morning. Instruct them to look all around for shadows. As they search, ask questions (such as those below) to help formulate ideas.

- Can you find a big shadow? Small shadow?
- Why is one shadow bigger/smaller than another?
- How are the shadows alike? Different?
- How are the shadows made? Can you make one?
- What will happen to a shadow outside at night? On a cloudy day?

Did You Know...

A shadow is a dark area that is caused when an object prevents light from shining on a surface. To make a shadow, there must be a light source and an object.

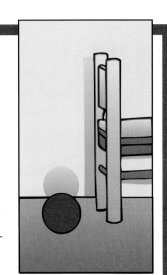

Shadow Center

This is the place for lots of discovery learning! Cover a small table or desk with a white cloth or white paper. Provide a set of one-inch blocks and a flashlight. As a small group visits this center, encourage the students to build a structure with the blocks. Then have them try to make shadows by moving the light source around the structure. (If necessary, dim the lights in that section of the room.) As children freely explore, guide them to discover the facts in the following "Did You Know...."

Did You Know...

You can change the length of the shadow by changing the angle of the light. By placing the light directly above the structure, you can even make the shadow disappear. A shadow is always opposite the light source. The direction of the shadow will change if the direction of the light source changes.

Pam Crane

Secret Shadows

To make secret shadows, you will need an overhead projector, a file folder (or two if needed), and a collection of opaque objects. In advance hide the objects in a box. Tape the file folder(s) around the base of the projector so your children will not be able to see the objects on the screen. Then gather your class. One at a time, place the objects on the screen and have children guess each object's identity based on the shadow that it casts. Begin with easily recognized items, such as a pair of scissors, a paper clip, and a key. Then progress to more difficult items, such as a button, a book, or a marble. The secret's out!

Don't Even Tell the Teacher!

Repeat the "Secret Shadows" activity with a twist—this time *you're* in the audience too! Invite children to secretly bring in items from home. Have each child, in turn, place his item on the shielded overhead projector. Then everybody tries to guess the object's identity by the shadow. Youngsters will be motivated to try to stump even the teacher!

To Shadow or Not to Shadow

Now it's time to delve further into the exploration of making shadows! To guide youngsters to discover that not all objects cast the same type of shadow, you'll need a flashlight, opaque objects (such as a piece of cardboard and a book), translucent objects (such as a piece of waxed paper and a tissue), and transparent objects (such as a piece of clear plastic wrap and a clean transparency). You'll also need a copy of page 65 for each child. To do this activity, put all of the objects and the reproducibles in a center. Ask each child to look at the objects one at a time. Have her predict whether each object will cast a shadow. Then encourage the child to see whether she can make a shadow using the flashlight and the object. Have her record the results on the chart. After each child has visited the center, come together as a group to discuss the results. (If you'd like to do this as a whole-group activity, simply enlarge and duplicate page 65 to make a large chart.)

Did You Know...

An opaque object does not allow light to pass through it, so it casts a dark shadow. A translucent (partly see-through) or transparent (completely see-through) object allows some light to pass through it, so its shadow is dimmer or sometimes not there at all.

The Literature Link

Geoffrey the groundhog provides a whimsical look at shadows in story form. Read aloud *Geoffrey Groundhog Predicts the Weather* by Bruce Koscielniak. After discussing the story with your class, invite each child to make a groundhog (see the directions below) for some fun shadow-making practice.

Groundhog Shadows

With groundhogs of their own, your youngsters will be able to experiment with shadows in groundhog style! In advance, collect several plastic, two-liter bottles. To make a groundhog, wrap a large sheet of construction paper around a two-liter bottle; then tape the paper closed. Use art supplies (such as construction paper, pom-poms, and markers) to decorate the paper tube to resemble a groundhog. When the groundhog is complete, slide it off the bottle. Encourage children to take their groundhogs outside on a sunny day and on a cloudy day. Then have them try making different kinds of shadows by moving their groundhogs around.

Name _____

Will it cast a shadow?

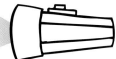

Object	Prediction	Result

©The Mailbox® • *Science* • TEC1493

Explorations

Dental Magic

There's magic in a healthy smile. Use this lesson to demonstrate the importance of toothbrushing every day.

STEP 1

In advance hard-boil a class supply of eggs plus one extra. Use a permanent marker to draw a toothy grin on an egg for each child. Also personalize a cup for each child.

STEP 2

During a group time, invite the children to share their dental health–related experiences, such as visits to a dentist, toothbrushing routines, or a sibling that lost a tooth. Draw a toothy grin on the extra egg. Then explain to the group that eggshells and teeth are made of the same material—calcium.

STEP 5

Suggest that since eggshells are similar to teeth, they can be cleaned in the same manner. Provide each child in the group with an old toothbrush. Working near a sink or tub of water, have the children use the brushes and toothpaste to clean their eggs.

STEP 6

Discuss the results. Remind your little ones that *all* of their teeth should be brushed every day to keep them clean and remove stains. Then sing the following song:

Brush Your Teeth
(sung to the tune of "Clementine")

Brush your front teeth;
Brush your back teeth;
Brush the bottom and the top.
If you brush them each and every day,
Then your smile will never stop.

Science You Can Do
by Suzanne Moore

To learn about keeping teeth clean, you will need the following:
hard-boiled egg for each child, plus one extra
black permanent marker
clear, plastic cup for each child
enough strong tea or caramel-colored soda to fill each child's cup
paper towels
spoon   toothpaste
old toothbrushes   a sink or tub of water

Note: Be sure children and adults wash their hands thoroughly after handling eggs.

STEP 3

Invite small groups of children at a time to join you in a science area. Direct each child to put an egg into his cup. Invite each child to pour tea or soda into his cup so that the egg is covered. (Do not put the extra egg in liquid.) Ask the group to predict what will happen if the eggs soak in the liquid overnight. Set the cups aside.

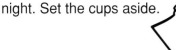

STEP 4

The next day invite small groups of children to join you again to observe the results of the experiment. Have each child use a spoon to remove his egg from the cup and dry the egg with a paper towel. Observe the changes in the eggshells by comparing them to the extra egg. Lead the group to conclude that the shells were stained by the liquid.

Did You Know?

- How does toothpaste clean the eggshells and our teeth? Toothpaste contains an abrasive substance—such as finely powdered chalk—and a detergent. Flavors are added to make the taste pleasant, and fluoride is added to help prevent decay.
- Baby teeth are important too! Dental decay that is not treated in primary teeth can spread to other teeth and even to the permanent teeth below the gum that have not yet emerged.
- Children begin to lose their baby teeth between the ages of five and seven. Permanent teeth are fully developed and will begin to erupt when the child is about six years old.

What Now?

Make old-fashioned toothpaste! Mix three parts baking soda with one part salt. To use, moisten a toothbrush; then coat it with the powder. Try scrubbing a stained egg with this paste. Which works better—the homemade paste or the commercial paste?

Chilly Science

Are you freezing this winter? Even if it is not cold where you live, your little ones will shiver with excitement when they complete these activities for freezing and melting!

ideas by Suzanne Moore

Icy-Cool Exploration

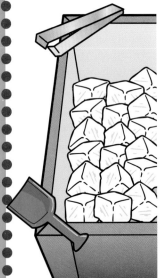

Surprise your young scientists with this icy investigation of a familiar substance—ice! In advance, wrap a cube-shaped box with white paper to resemble an ice cube. Label a different side of the cube with one of the following words: *looks, feels, sounds,* or *smells.* Pour a bag or two of ice into your empty water table or a large plastic container. Provide pairs of rubber gloves (to protect little hands), hand lenses, plastic containers, tongs, and plastic shovels. Invite small groups of youngsters to investigate the ice; encourage them to think about how the ice looks, feels, sounds, and smells. After everyone has had a chance to explore the ice and it has begun to melt, ask students to describe the experience. Write students' responses on the appropriate side of the box. After discussing student observations, explain that ice is water that has frozen solid. It melts—changes back into water—when it is surrounded by warmth. The warmth of the air in the classroom and of students' hands will change the ice into water. Brrr!

DID YOU KNOW?
When water freezes, it expands and increases in volume by about $\frac{1}{11}$.

Freeze!

Now that students have experienced ice melting into water, they'll be ready to discover what happens when water freezes. Place a funnel in a half-gallon plastic jug; then enlist youngsters' help in filling the jug with water. When the jug is full, replace the cap. Next, wrap a length of yarn around the middle of the jug and then cut the yarn where it meets itself. Place the jug in a freezer overnight. The next day, remove the jug from the freezer. Invite students to observe the jug. Lead students to discuss the changes that occurred when the water inside the jug froze. Use the same length of yarn to measure around the middle of the jug. Discuss any change in size with your youngsters. Remove the cap from the jug and have students observe the ice. Explain to students that when water freezes it expands and that this expansion caused the ice to make the sides of the jug bulge and the cap come up. Cool discovery!

The Great Ice Race

Which type of ice will melt more quickly, crushed ice or a solid block? Your youngsters will ponder this question and find the answer with this simple experiment. To prepare, freeze an eight-ounce paper cup of water. You will also need eight ounces of crushed ice. Remove the frozen water from the cup and place it in an aluminum pie pan. In a separate pan, spread the crushed ice in a single layer. Place a sheet of paper and a marker beside each pan. Invite each child to predict which pan of ice will melt first by writing his name on the appropriate paper. Set a timer and have your youngsters observe the ice every ten minutes. After one pan of ice has melted completely, discuss students' predictions and the experiment results. Then explain to students that because the crushed ice was spread over a greater surface area, each small piece of ice came in contact with the warmer air temperature in the classroom, making it melt more quickly. A chilly conclusion!

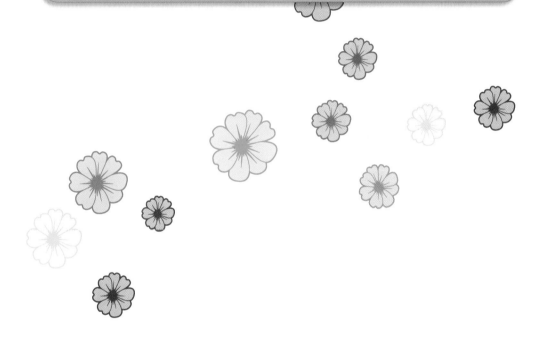

Spring Science

Bring On Spring Weather!

Rain or shine, your young meteorologists will love these springtime weather activities!

ideas by Suzanne Moore

Observing Predicting

Weather Watchers

Turn your little ones into weather forecasters with these five-day observation and forecast booklets. Make a class set of page 74. Give each youngster a copy and have her cut out the booklet pages along the dashed cut lines. Instruct each child to apply glue to her forecast page where indicated and then place her observation page on top. After the glue has dried, have each child write her name on the front of her booklet.

On Monday, have each student observe the weather and then draw a picture to represent it on the first flap. Then ask her to lift the flap and predict tomorrow's weather by circling the appropriate word and illustration. On Tuesday, after weather observations for the day have been made, have students discuss whether their predictions from the previous day were correct. Continue observing and forecasting the weather for the remainder of the week.

At the end of the week, have your young meteorologists look over the week's observations and talk about how the weather changed.

Did you know?

Spring weather is not really hot or cold. Warm air and cool air mix during spring, making the air unsettled. This unsettled air can cause strong thunderstorms, hail, and tornadoes.

Language

We Love Spring Weather

Teach your youngsters this little ditty; then sing up a storm! Sing an additional verse by replacing the underlined word with the word *sun*.

(sung to the tune of "For He's a Jolly Good Fellow")

We love the [rain] in the springtime.
We love the [rain] in the springtime.
We love the [rain] in the springtime.
It helps all Earth's plants grow!

It helps all Earth's plants grow!
It helps all Earth's plants grow!
We love the [rain] in the springtime.
It helps all Earth's plants grow!

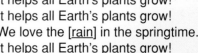

Drip...Drop...Raindrops!

The next time it rains, try this interesting demonstration to investigate the size of raindrops. To prepare, fill the bottom of an aluminum pie pan with one inch of flour. Level the flour with the back of a spoon. While it's raining, hold the pan in the rain for a few seconds. You'll see that you have captured raindrops. Invite youngsters to observe that the raindrops have formed pellets. Let the pellets dry for an hour. Then carefully remove them from the pan with tweezers and place them on a sheet of black construction paper. Have students use hand lenses to observe the pellets. Lead students to discover that the size of the pellets is determined by the size of the raindrops. What a great way to brighten the dreariest of rainy spring days!

Did you know?

When raindrops hit the ground, they bounce. The harder the surface, the higher the raindrops bounce.

Following directions
Movement

Puddle Jumpers

What does spring rain leave behind? Puddles! In advance, cut a four-foot length of brown yarn for each child. Read aloud David McPhail's *The Puddle.* Then have students discuss their experiences of playing outdoors after it has rained. Next, invite your little ones to do some puddle jumping of their own. Give each child a length of yarn and have him form it into a puddle shape on the floor. Have youngsters listen and follow directions as you give commands such as "Walk around your puddle, jump over it, tiptoe through it, or sit in it." Ahhh, mess-free puddle play!

Graphing

So Many Umbrellas

Here's a home-school activity that will help reinforce graphing skills and create a nice bulletin board display too! Make a class set of the bottom half of page 73. Send one copy of the note home with each child. Cover a bulletin board with light blue paper and copy the poem from the parent note in the center of the board. After the umbrella pictures have been returned to school, instruct students to cut out their umbrellas. Have youngsters sort the umbrella pictures by color or pattern. Label your bulletin board similar to the one shown, including the umbrella categories needed to complete your class graph. Have each child tape his umbrella to the board in the appropriate column. Then discuss the graph results.

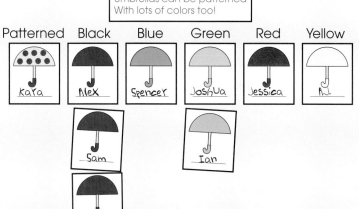

71

Spring Wind Blows

Teach your little performers this chant to help them start thinking about wind.

The spring wind blows this way and that.
Oops! Watch out! There goes my hat!

Wave hands above head.

The spring wind blows round and round.
It blows my hat across the ground.

Move arms in a rolling motion.

The spring wind blows. Spin, spin, spin!
Oops, it blows my hat again!

Move hand in a circular upward motion.

The spring wind blows left and right.
Then it blows my hat out of sight!

Move hands to the left, then right.
Wave bye-bye.

Did you know?

Wind is air on the move. Wind is caused when warm air and cool air change places.

Blowing in the Wind

Windsocks are a great way to discover which direction the wind is blowing and its strength. Make these clever windsocks and encourage your students to take them outside to help determine the wind's intensity and direction. To make a windsock, give each child a gallon-size resealable plastic bag and have him cut along the bottom edge. Then instruct him to fringe-cut the bottom of the bag so that each fringe piece is about one inch wide and four inches long. Hole-punch through both thicknesses near the top of each child's bag to make two holes. Then tie each end of an 18-inch length of yarn through a different hole to make a hanger. Invite each child to use permanent markers and stickers to decorate his windsock. Then take the windsocks outside to check for windy conditions.

Sunshine or Shade?

Help your students understand the sun's warming effect with this simple experiment. Put several chocolate chips in each of two aluminum pie pans. Place one pan in a sunny spot on your playground and the other pan in a shady spot. Then have students make predictions about what will happen to the chocolate chips in each pan. Record student responses on a chart as shown. Wait 30 minutes and have students check the chips. Record their observations. Explain to students that because an object (tree, slide, etc.) created shade, it blocked some of the sun's heat, therefore making the chips in the shade less likely to melt.

In shade	In sunshine
I think they will stay the same. Cara	I think they will turn into blobs. Alex
I think they will stay hard. Tim	I think they will melt. Keesha

Pam Crane

Solar Snacks

Put the sun to work heating some tasty snacks with the help of these easy-to-make solar ovens. In advance, collect a shoebox for each child. Distribute the boxes and have each youngster line the inside of her box with aluminum foil. Then gather the ingredients listed below and help each youngster assemble her snack. Place the child's snack in her solar oven. Cover the top of the box with plastic wrap; then secure the overlapping edges with tape. Put the solar ovens in a very sunny place and heat the snacks for about two hours. Check the snacks often and eat them once they are heated.

Ingredients for one:
$\frac{1}{2}$ graham cracker (two sections)
square of chocolate
large marshmallow

Directions:
1. Stack the chocolate and marshmallow on one graham cracker half.
2. Heat.
3. Eat!

- -

Parent Note
Use with "So Many Umbrellas" on page 71.

_____
name

Umbrellas

Umbrellas can be red.
Umbrellas can be blue.
Umbrellas can be patterned
With lots of colors too!

Dear Parent,

Have your child look at your umbrella. Talk about its color and pattern, if any. Then have your child color the umbrella picture to the left to resemble the real one. (If you don't have an umbrella at home, have your child color the umbrella picture any way he or she wishes.) Return this sheet to school by _____.

Thank you!

Weather Booklet

Use with "Weather Watchers" on page 70.

_____, Weather Watcher

©The Mailbox®

Monday's Weather Observation	Tuesday's Weather Observation	Wednesday's Weather Observation	Thursday's Weather Observation	Friday's Weather Observation

Add glue.

Tuesday's weather will be...
sunny
rainy
windy

Wednesday's weather will be...
sunny
rainy
windy

Thursday's weather will be...
sunny
rainy
windy

Friday's weather will be...
sunny
rainy
windy

Saturday's weather will be...
sunny
rainy
windy

Beautiful Butterflies

Use these activities to teach your little learners about the factual side of beautiful butterflies!

adapted from ideas by Judy Pilcher

From Egg to Adult

This cute craft will help your students learn about the life cycle of a butterfly. In advance, prepare a paper plate for each child by using a marker to divide each one into four equal sections and labeling each section as shown. Then explain to students that a butterfly goes through four different stages to become an adult butterfly. First, an *egg* is laid. When the egg hatches, the *larva*, or *caterpillar*, emerges. The caterpillar eats lots of food and grows. Next, it attaches itself to a twig or leaf and a hard covering forms. During this stage it is called a *pupa*. While inside the covering, the pupa changes and then emerges as an adult butterfly.

Distribute the plates and guide each youngster in using an ink pad to make prints on his plate to complete each section as shown. Next, invite him to add details to his butterfly life cycle with crayons or markers. Display the projects on a bulletin board titled "Butterflies: From Egg to Adult."

1. egg	2. larva
3. pupa	4. adult

DID YOU KNOW?
There are between 15,000 and 20,000 different kinds of butterflies! Wow!

Build a Butterfly

Have your youngsters put together these tasty treats to review butterfly body parts. To prepare, use clean kitchen shears to cut one small flour tortilla into butterfly-shaped wings, as shown,

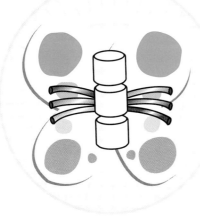

for each child. Tint corn syrup with food coloring to make several different colors. Cut six 1½" lengths of licorice lace (legs) for each youngster. Provide each child with a paper plate, a plastic spoon, three large marshmallows (*head, thorax,* and *abdomen*), wings, legs, and access to tinted corn syrup. Then have each student use her spoon to paint her wings with corn syrup. Instruct her to add a head, thorax, and abdomen to the center of the wings. Next, have her insert six legs into the thorax. Review the butterfly body parts; then have your little ones eat up!

Sipping Up Nectar

This simple activity helps your students understand how a butterfly eats. In advance, gather a small paper cup and straw for each child. Cut a construction paper flower that is two inches larger in diameter than the mouth of the cup; then make two cuts in the center of the flower as shown. Slip a flower onto each cup and tape it in place. Explain to students that most butterflies feed on nectar through a long sucking tube called a *proboscis*. Give each child a straw and a flower cup containing a small amount of juice. Then invite each youngster to use his proboscis (straw) to sip some nectar just like a real butterfly!

Read aloud *Waiting for Wings* by Lois Ehlert.

Wonders Never Cease
Simple Science for Young Children

I can turn my head toward the sun.

Living and Nonliving Things

Use the ideas in this unit to enter into the study of one of the most fundamental concepts of all scientific classifications—living and nonliving things.

ideas contributed by Ann Flagg

Objective: Students will learn to identify living and nonliving things. Students will be able to identify three basic life processes of all living things—eating, growing, and moving.

The Basics

Introduce the topic of living and nonliving things to your students by reading aloud *What's Alive?* by Kathleen Weidner Zoehfeld. With elementary text and charming illustrations, this title from the Let's-Read-and-Find-Out Science series presents solid science information at a level that is just right for early childhood. After discussing the book, guide your youngsters to verbalize the characteristics of living things mentioned in the book; then write them on the board. *(All living things take in food, grow, and move by themselves.)* With those three characteristics in mind, revisit the illustrations in the book. Call attention to random pictures in the book, asking youngsters whether they are living or nonliving things and why. (For example, on pages 4 and 5 of the book, you could ask about the chair, the doll, the cat, the dog, the ball, the teddy bear, and the cut flowers. The flowers might require some interesting discussion!)

Observation

Take your class on a walk around your school grounds. Prompt youngsters to look for things that are alive and things that are not alive. Carry a whistle with you and use it to call everyone together at interesting stops. Also draw youngsters' attention to contrasting items such as live leaves on a tree and dead leaves on the ground. Encourage discussion about each of these items; then return to your classroom for the next activity.

Would you like a sandwich?

Pam Crane

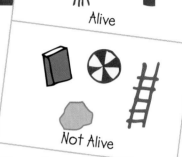

Recording Information

Back in the classroom, give each child a large sheet of paper and instruct him to fold it in half. Have him title one half "Alive" and the other half "Not Alive." Encourage each child to remember several things that he saw on the walk and then illustrate each of his ideas on the appropriate side of the paper. Afterward, have each child share his page with the group. (If a child decides that he has misplaced one of his drawings, he can rectify the placement in "Classification.")

Classification

Now that your youngsters have thought about the idea of living and nonliving, go one step further into classification. Using bulletin board border, divide a board into two vertical sections, with one side being larger than the other (as shown). Title the large side of the board "Living" and the other side "Nonliving." Then subtitle the "Living" side "Plants" and "Animals." Have each child cut out his pictures from "Recording Information." Then review page 30 of *What's Alive?*, asking youngsters to follow the directions in the book. Have each child pin or staple his pictures in the appropriate places on the board. (Note: If you don't have a copy of *What's Alive?*, have each child sort his pictures into living and nonliving things. Next, ask him to sort the living things into *plants* and *animals* and then mount the pictures on the board.)

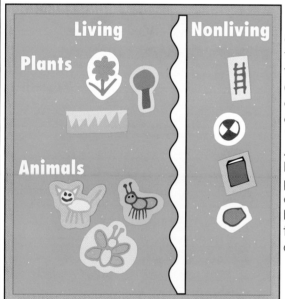

I'm Alive!

Delight your students with a look at some of the most "alive-ly" things around—themselves! Duplicate pages 78 and 79 for each child; then cut apart the pages. Follow the directions below for each page. Then have each child color the cover and write her name on it. Complete the booklet by having the child sequence the cover and the pages; then help her staple the booklet together along the left edge. Encourage children to share these very lively booklets with their families.

Page 1: Read the text together. Have each child draw and label some of her favorite things to eat.

Page 2: Read the text together. Have each child trace her hand in the space provided and then write her age in the blank.

Page 3: Read the text together. Have each child illustrate herself doing one of her favorite movement activities.

I'm Alive!

by _____

©The Mailbox® • Science • TEC1493

I'm alive!

I eat...

1

I'm alive!
I am growing.

This is a baby's hand.   This is my hand at age _____.

2

I'm alive!
I can move by myself.

I eat. I'm growing. And I can move.
Yes, I'm alive!

3

Our Fine-Feathered Friends

Birds are in the country. Birds are in the city. Birds are in your own backyard. Think about it—birds are probably the most common wild animal that your youngsters see. So use these naturally occurring experiences combined with the ideas in this unit to take a fine-feathered flight into avian studies. You'll find a nestful of science along with reading and language, math, movement, and more.

ideas contributed by Lucia Kemp Henry

Bird Watching

What exactly *is* a bird? Pose this question to your youngsters and write their responses on a sheet of chart paper. Then launch your students into bird research. First, designate an area of your classroom (or playground) from which children can watch birds. Stock the area with a supply of paper, pencils, crayons, and a pair of binoculars (if available). Also fill your reading area with a variety of bird books (see the list in this unit). Next, introduce your children to the basics of bird watching with a reading of *Counting Is for the Birds* by Frank Mazzola Jr. Afterward, invite children to observe birds from the bird-watching station and by examining the books in your reading area. Encourage children to record their observations by writing or drawing. Then have each child share his findings with the class. Add any new information to your original list; then bind each child's research page into a class book.

- Birds are animals.
- All birds have feathers.
- All birds have wings.
- All birds have two legs and two wings.
- All birds have beaks.
- Most birds can fly.
- All birds hatch from eggs.

Seth

I saw a bird hopping.

The Bird Basics

Enhance your youngsters' understanding of birds by taking a thoughtful glimpse into the world of birds with *About Birds: A Guide for Children* by Cathryn Sill. Simple text and detailed illustrations skillfully provide a young audience with important information about birds.

Did You Know?

There are more than 9,000 different kinds of birds! How many can you name?

Here, Birdie, Birdie, Birdie!

Do those fine-feathered friends in your area require some enticement in order to be enjoyed at close range? Or perhaps your local bird population could use some help making it through a cold winter. Many types of birds can be attracted with simple bird feeders. The more kinds of food you offer, the more types of birds you are likely to see. (Check out some of the menu items to the right.) One of the simplest ways to attract a variety of birds is with sunflower seeds. You can offer these seeds in a variety of ways (see below) to attract an assortment of guests. It will be a pleasure serving these little diners, and they're sure to come back again!

Bird Favorites

- commercial birdseed
- cracked corn
- white millet
- suet (animal fat)
- sunflower seeds
- peanut butter
- peanut butter mixed with cornmeal (to prevent it from sticking to the bird's mouth in warm weather)
- roasted peanuts (in the shells)
  Note: Raw peanuts are not good for birds.

Bird Feeders

Cut holes in the sides of a clean plastic bottle. Poke holes in the bottom for drainage. Fill the bottom with seeds; then hang the feeder from a branch.

Many small birds will eat seeds from a shallow bowl.

Some birds prefer open platforms. Stabilize a piece of plywood on a sturdy bucket or garbage can; then scatter seeds on the platform.

Some ground-feeding birds come most readily to seeds scattered on the ground.

Suet (fat trimmings) can provide birds with essential fats. If it's cold, scrape suet onto pinecones; then hang the pinecones from trees. (If the temperatures are above freezing, raw suet spoils quickly. A longer-lasting form is available from stores that sell birdseed.)

Helpful Hint: Set up your feeders on a weekend or holiday when birds can discover them in relative peace. Then when the hustle and bustle of children resumes, the birds are more likely to continue visiting the feeders.

My Book About Birds

Your little readers will be proud to share their knowledge of birds after they've made their very own bird books. For each child, reproduce pages 84–89 on white construction paper. Provide scissors, glue, and crayons. (For variety, you might also like to provide colored pencils and watercolor paints.) As youngsters work on each page, invite them to peruse the books in your reading area to gather more information as needed. When the books are completed, read them together, having each child share his last page individually. Then encourage each youngster to take his book home to share with his family.

Features of the Creatures

A little rhythm and rhyme in the poem below helps reinforce the basic bird features. Copy the poem onto a large sheet of chart paper. Then read the poem aloud, encouraging children to join in and add motions as they are able. (There are lots of opportunities here to work with those beginning readers!) When youngsters are familiar with the poem, place the chart in your art area during center time. Invite children to visit the center and help decorate the border around the poem.

All About Birds
Birds are very special creatures
With very special "bird-y" features.
Instead of arms, birds have two wings.
And those are just two "bird-y" things!

Birds have beautiful feathers too,
Instead of hair like me and you.
Each bird has a beak instead of a nose.
And each bird has special "bird-y" type toes!

Birds build the nests that suit them best.
Then Mama lays eggs in her special bird nest.
And birds live almost everywhere—
On water, on land, and in the air!

Wings, feathers, beaks, and toes:
You might see them all—who knows?
So be on the lookout for these creatures
With all these special "bird-y" features.

Pam Crane

Bird Books

Eyewitness Books: *Bird* by David Burnie
Counting Is for the Birds by Frank Mazzola Jr.
Feathers for Lunch by Lois Ehlert
Sky Dancer by Jack Bushnell

Birds the World Over

With more than 9,000 types of birds in existence, where must they all live? Your little ornithologists might be quite surprised to find out the answer: just about everywhere! In advance, cut out a supply of small construction paper birds. Then begin a class discussion about where birds live by looking through *Have You Seen Birds?* by Joanne T. Oppenheim. For each different bird habitat mentioned, attach a bird cutout to a map or globe to create a visual representation of where birds live. Guide your students to summarize that birds are all over the world!

Classroom Roosts

Have your youngsters ever thought about birds in the city? *Urban Roosts* by Barbara Bash offers new insight into how many birds might actually be roosting right under (or above!) the noses of the average city dwellers! After a reading of *Urban Roosts,* reinforce what students have learned by having them design classroom roosts for their own child-created birds. To begin, have each child sculpt a bird from modeling clay. Then have each child search the room and place his bird in the roosting place of his choice. When all birds are roosting, have the children gather together on your rug. From where they're sitting, see how many birds your youngsters can spot. Encourage children to describe each bird's roost using a variety of position words. Can they spot all the birds? (Save the birds for the next activity.)

Home, "Tweet" Home

In joyful P. D. Eastman style, *The Best Nest* brings home the old adage "home is where the heart is." After sharing this delightful tale with your youngsters, encourage children to design nests/homes for their clay birds (from "Classroom Roosts") that are realistic or imaginary! Provide supplies such as construction paper, strawberry baskets, small boxes, yarn, ribbon, fabric scraps, clay, cotton, and dried grasses. Refer children to your collection of fiction and nonfiction bird books and then let them have at it! Encourage each child to share his finished project with the class, telling whether he thinks his nest resembles a real or imaginary bird home.

Book Cover
Use with "My Book About Birds" on page 82.

My Book About

Birds

wren

Glue wing here

by _____

©The Mailbox® • Science • TEC1493

Color.

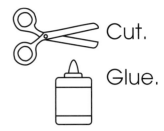
Cut.

Glue.

1

chickadee

Glue wing here.

Birds have wings.

Color.

Cut.

Glue.

Book Page 2

Use with "My Book About Birds" on page 82.

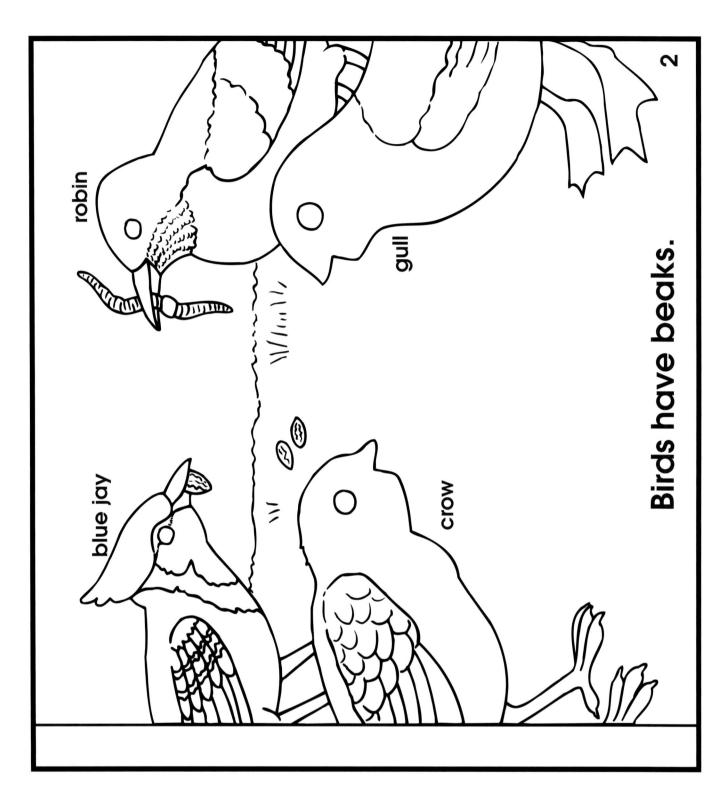

robin

gull

blue jay

crow

Birds have beaks.

2

Draw beaks for the crow and gull.

Color.

3

cardinal

Glue
tail here.

Birds have feathers.

Color.
Cut.
Glue.

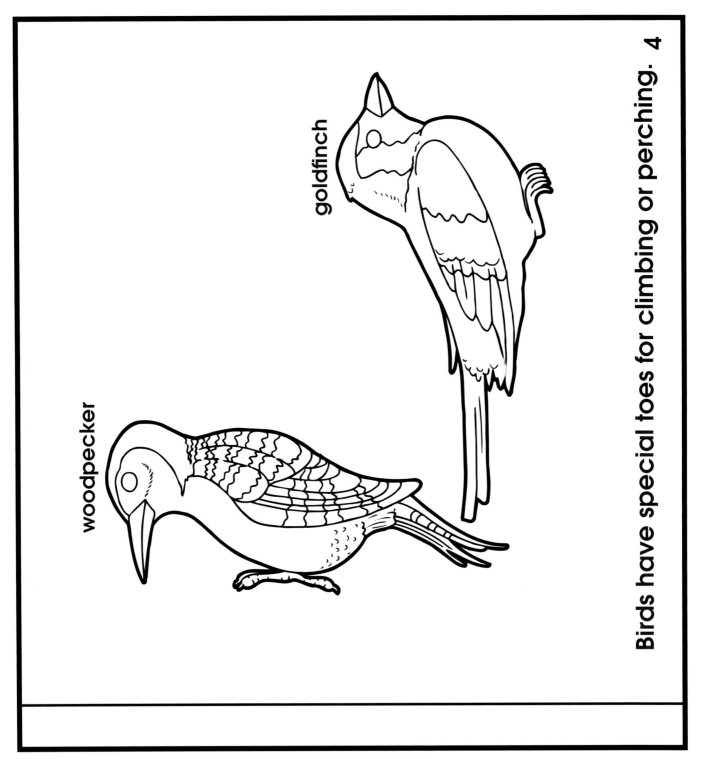

goldfinch

woodpecker

Birds have special toes for climbing or perching. 4

Draw a tree for the woodpecker.

Draw a branch for the goldfinch.

Color.

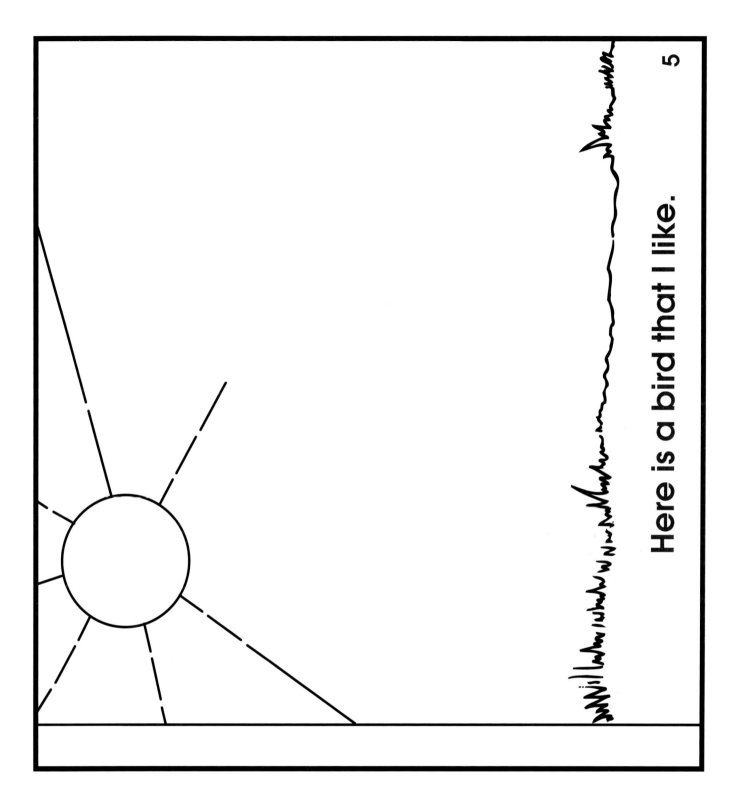

5

Here is a bird that I like.

Draw.

Color.

Wonders Never Cease
Simple Science for Young Children

Investigating Eggs

Scramble up some scientific thinking with these egg explorations.

ideas by Dr. Suzanne Moore

Note: Be sure both children and adults wash their hands thoroughly after handling eggs.

What We Know
• Eggs are white.
• Some are brown and blue too.
• Eggs crack.
• These eggs are cold and smooth.

What We Want To Know
• What happens to the baby chick?
• When the mom chicken sits on the eggs, why don't they crack?

What Do You Know?

Introduce your youngsters to egg investigations by posing the following riddle: What must be broken before it can be used? When someone guesses an egg—with your prompting, if necessary—pass around a few hard-boiled eggs. Ask youngsters to carefully examine the eggs and tell what they already know about them. Write children's responses on an egg-shaped cutout. Then ask what your youngsters would like to know about eggs. Write these queries on a different egg-shaped cutout. At the culmination of your egg studies, write a list of what your students learned on a third egg-shaped cutout. So that's what you know!

shell
white
yolk
Joey

Three in One

How many parts does an egg have? Crack open this mystery and see! Give each child in a small group a sheet of paper. Display a raw egg; then ask students how many parts they think the egg has. Then break open the egg (being careful not to break the yolk) and pour the insides onto a plate. Also position the eggshells on the plate. Pass the plate around, encouraging the children to visually examine the egg and then draw what they see. How many parts did they draw? Summarize your discussion by writing the actual names of each egg part: white, yolk, and shell. Have each child copy the words on the appropriate part of his illustration. Then encourage each child to take his illustration home and share this information with his family.

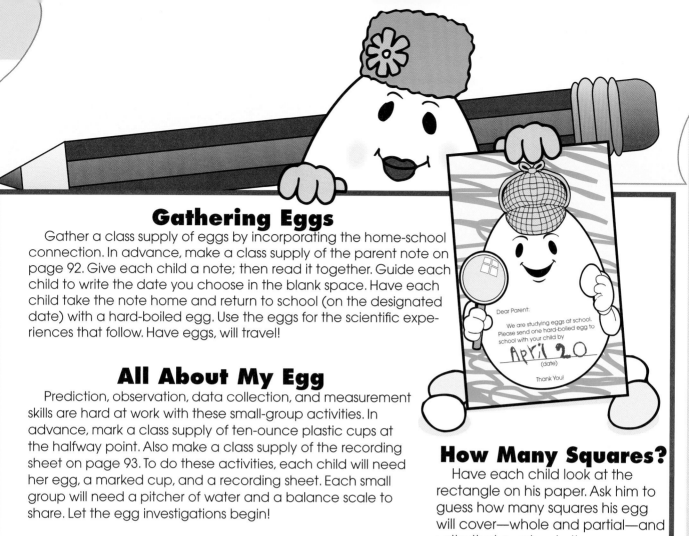

Gathering Eggs

Gather a class supply of eggs by incorporating the home-school connection. In advance, make a class supply of the parent note on page 92. Give each child a note; then read it together. Guide each child to write the date you choose in the blank space. Have each child take the note home and return to school (on the designated date) with a hard-boiled egg. Use the eggs for the scientific experiences that follow. Have eggs, will travel!

All About My Egg

Prediction, observation, data collection, and measurement skills are hard at work with these small-group activities. In advance, mark a class supply of ten-ounce plastic cups at the halfway point. Also make a class supply of the recording sheet on page 93. To do these activities, each child will need her egg, a marked cup, and a recording sheet. Each small group will need a pitcher of water and a balance scale to share. Let the egg investigations begin!

How Much Space?

Help each child fill her cup to the mark with water. Have her color in the bottom half of the cup on her recording sheet with a blue crayon. Then have each child gently place her egg in the water. What happens to the water? Invite children to share their observations and to brainstorm why the water level changed. After your discussion, explain that the egg and the water cannot take up the same space at the same time. So the egg pushed the water out of the way. Have children record the new water level with another color of crayon.

How Much Weight?

Have each child, in turn, position his egg on one side of a balance scale. Then have him add small blocks or counters to the other side until the scale is balanced. Encourage each child to complete his recording sheet by drawing the objects on the scale and filling in the blank under the scale.

How Many Squares?

Have each child look at the rectangle on his paper. Ask him to guess how many squares his egg will cover—whole and partial—and write that number in the space provided. Next, have him place his egg on the graphed rectangle and trace around it. Then have him remove his egg and count the number of squares within the egg shape. Instruct him to write that number on his recording sheet; then discuss the differences.

Parent Note

Use with "Gathering Eggs" on page 91.

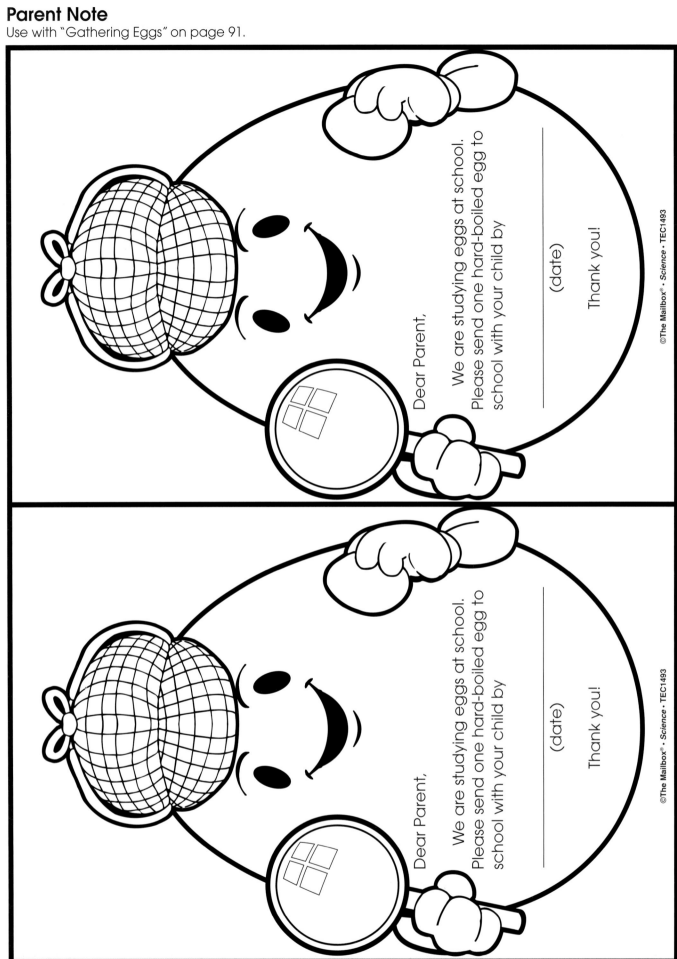

Dear Parent,

We are studying eggs at school.
Please send one hard-boiled egg to
school with your child by

_____
(date)

Thank you!

©The Mailbox® • *Science* • TEC1493

Dear Parent,

We are studying eggs at school.
Please send one hard-boiled egg to
school with your child by

_____
(date)

Thank you!

©The Mailbox® • *Science* • TEC1493

All About My Egg

by _____

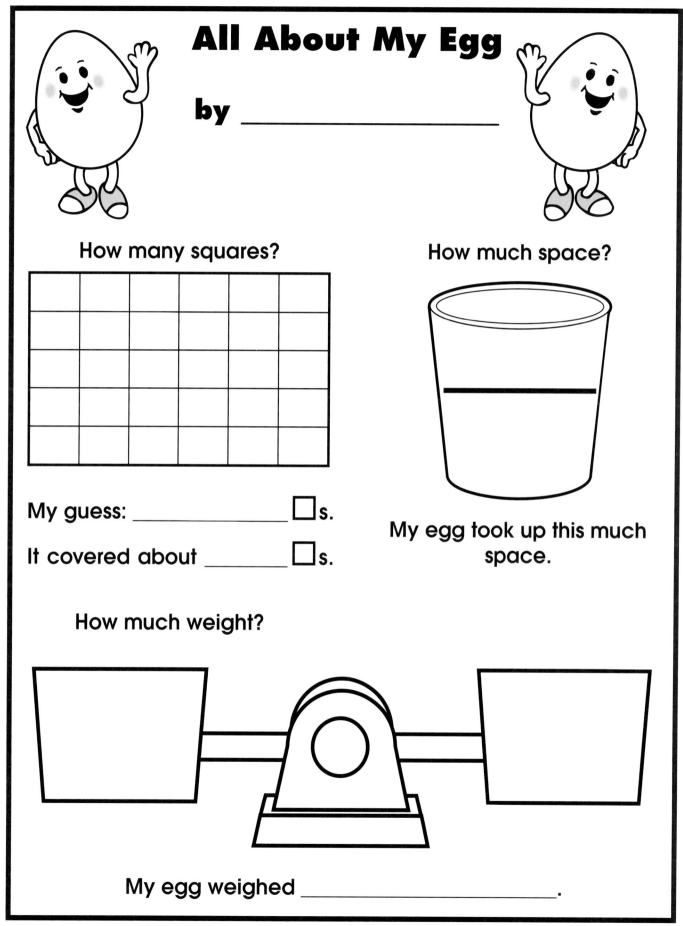

How many squares?

How much space?

My guess: _____ ☐s.

It covered about _____ ☐s.

My egg took up this much space.

How much weight?

My egg weighed _____.

PLANT PARTS MADE SIMPLE

Plant science is as simple as A, B, C with this child-friendly collection of observations, investigations, and experiments.

by Lucia Kemp Henry

Predicting

A SCIENCE MYSTERY

Make the most of your students' budding interest in science with this mystery activity. Several days before the activity, purchase a tomato seedling from your local plant nursery. Make several small holes in the bottom of an eight-ounce clear plastic cup for drainage. Add soil to the cup and then plant the seedling. Keep the cup on a sunny windowsill at home, watering the seedling regularly. Once a few roots begin to peek through the soil around the sides of the cup, bring the plant to school. Secretly place the plant in a large grocery bag. Lead youngsters to discuss what is inside the bag. Then read the clues listed below, pausing after each one to allow time for guessing. After students have identified the object as a plant, remove it from the bag for students to study and discuss.

What is in the bag?
- It is something we can study.
- It is in soil.
- It is alive.
- It grows.
- It is green.
- It has leaves.

Defining

THE PARTS OF PLANTS

Sing this song to help your budding botanists learn basic plant parts. To prepare, make a copy of the plant part patterns on page 98. Color and cut out the patterns. Then glue felt to the back of each pattern piece to prepare it for flannelboard use. Display each pattern piece as students sing the accompanying verse of the song below.

(sung to the tune of "The Farmer in the Dell")

A seed grows little roots.
A seed grows little roots.
The roots grow down into the soil.
A seed grows little roots.

A seed grows a long stem.
A seed grows a long stem.
The stem grows way up toward the sun.
A seed grows a long stem.

A plant grows many leaves.
A plant grows many leaves.
The leaves grow out quite green and strong.
A plant grows many leaves.

A plant can grow a flower.
A plant can grow a flower.
The flower grows and holds the seeds.
A plant can grow a flower.

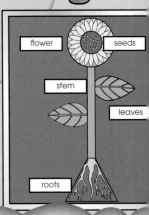

Leafy Learning

Focus your youngsters' attention on the similarities and differences of a variety of leaves with this activity. In advance, collect a variety of leaves so that each child can observe two different kinds. Copy page 99 to make a class set. Distribute the copies and then have each child select two different leaves. Instruct each student to choose crayons that match the color of each leaf. Next, demonstrate how to use a crayon to make a leaf rubbing. Then have each student make rubbings of his leaves on his paper. Instruct him to study his rubbings and his actual leaves to look for similarities and differences between the two types of leaves. Then help each child write his comparisons on his paper where indicated. "Be-leaf-able" fun!

Name Kent

My Leaves

Comparing leaves

Leaf A

Leaf B

Stem Science

Use this super-duper demonstration to help your youngsters discover why the stem of a plant is so important. To prepare, gather a 1" x 4½" strip of a thick white paper towel, a craft stick, a clothespin, and a clear 16-ounce plastic cup containing water tinted with blue food coloring. Use the clothespin to clip one end of the paper towel strip to the center of the craft stick. Review with students the parts of a plant. Explain that the stem is important because water moves through it to other parts of the plant. Display the paper towel strip and have students predict what will happen when you dip the end of the strip in the water. Place the craft stick across the top of the rim of the cup so that the strip touches the water. Have students observe the strip. After it is completely wet, lead students to conclude that water can move up the stem of a plant like the water moved up the paper towel strip. Super stem science!

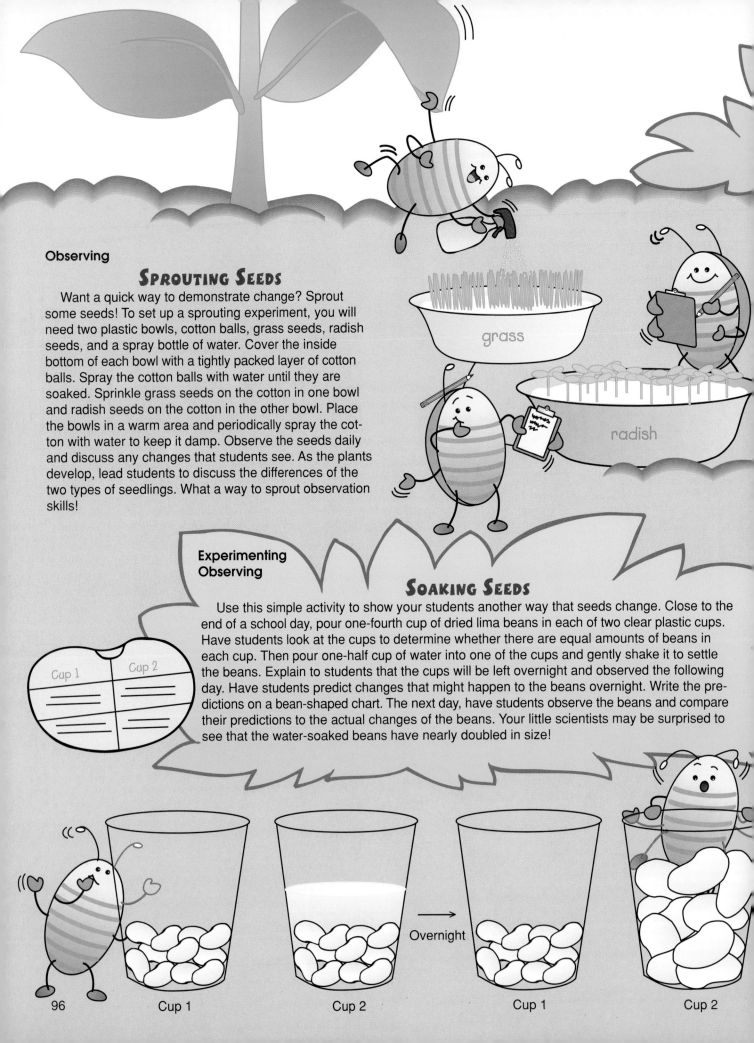

Observing

SPROUTING SEEDS

Want a quick way to demonstrate change? Sprout some seeds! To set up a sprouting experiment, you will need two plastic bowls, cotton balls, grass seeds, radish seeds, and a spray bottle of water. Cover the inside bottom of each bowl with a tightly packed layer of cotton balls. Spray the cotton balls with water until they are soaked. Sprinkle grass seeds on the cotton in one bowl and radish seeds on the cotton in the other bowl. Place the bowls in a warm area and periodically spray the cotton with water to keep it damp. Observe the seeds daily and discuss any changes that students see. As the plants develop, lead students to discuss the differences of the two types of seedlings. What a way to sprout observation skills!

grass

radish

Experimenting
Observing

SOAKING SEEDS

Use this simple activity to show your students another way that seeds change. Close to the end of a school day, pour one-fourth cup of dried lima beans in each of two clear plastic cups. Have students look at the cups to determine whether there are equal amounts of beans in each cup. Then pour one-half cup of water into one of the cups and gently shake it to settle the beans. Explain to students that the cups will be left overnight and observed the following day. Have students predict changes that might happen to the beans overnight. Write the predictions on a bean-shaped chart. The next day, have students observe the beans and compare their predictions to the actual changes of the beans. Your little scientists may be surprised to see that the water-soaked beans have nearly doubled in size!

Cup 1   Cup 2

Cup 1

Cup 2

Overnight

Cup 1

Cup 2

Planting seeds

GROW, PLANTS, GROW!

Give your little ones an inside look at plant growth with this activity. To prepare, gather the materials listed below and then guide each child through the directions to complete his own mini garden. As the plants grow, have students identify the plants' parts from roots to flowers.

Materials needed for one garden:
8 oz. clear plastic cup
8 oz. opaque plastic cup
potting soil
gravel
2 soaked lima beans (from "Soaking Seeds" on page 96)
water

Directions:
1. Add a small amount of gravel to the clear cup.
2. Add potting soil to nearly fill the cup.
3. Push a bean down along the inside of the cup so it can be seen from the outside. Repeat with the second bean on the opposite side of the cup.
4. Water the seeds.
5. Place the clear cup inside the opaque cup.
6. Place the cup in a sunny place.
7. Each day, remove the outer cup to observe changes and growth.

BOOKS TO GROW ON!

Use this crop of books to help your students' understanding of how plants sprout and grow!

THE REASON FOR A FLOWER
by
Ruth Heller

PLANTS AND FLOWERS (IT'S SCIENCE!)
by
Sally Hewitt

A DANDELION'S LIFE
by John Himmel-man

HOW A SEED GROWS (LET'S-READ-AND-FIND-OUT BOOKS)
by
Helene J. Jordan

FROM SEED TO PLANT
by
Gail Gibbons

Plant Part Patterns
Use with "The Parts of Plants" on page 94.

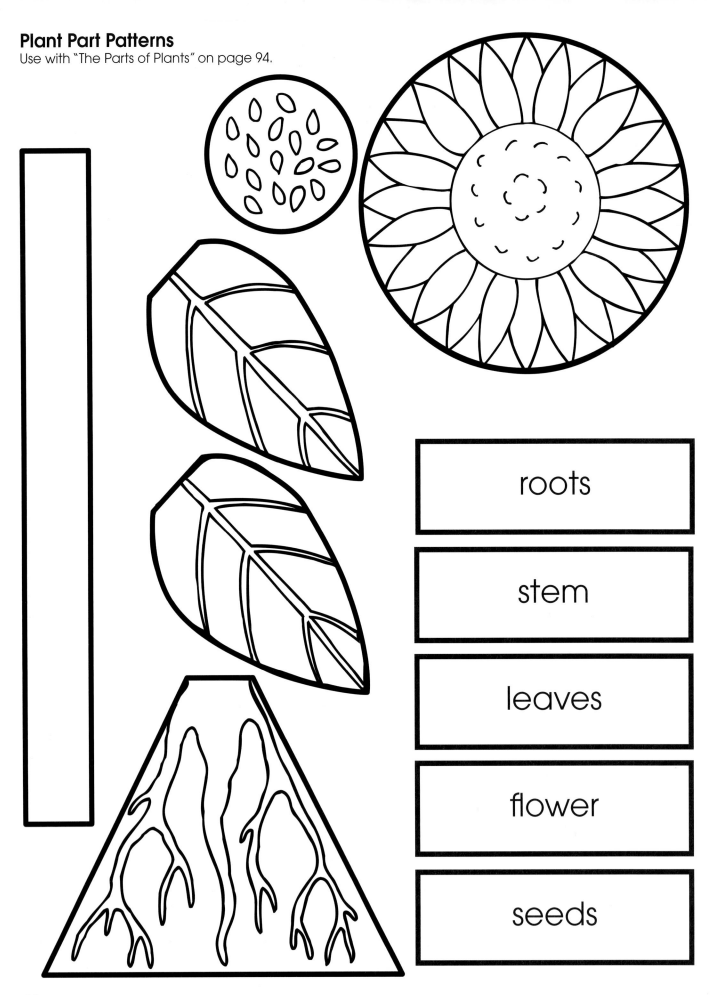

roots

stem

leaves

flower

seeds

MY LEAVES

Make a rubbing of each leaf.
Complete each sentence.

Leaf A	Leaf B

My leaves are alike because

_____

_____

My leaves are different because

_____

_____

©The Mailbox® • Science • TEC1493

Wonders Never Cease
Simple Science For Young Children

Digging Into Soil

It's a dirty job, but somebody's gotta do it. And your youngsters will be only too happy to oblige! So check out these soil-related activities to help your students dig into some nitty-gritty science.

ideas by Dr. Suzanne Moore

Objective: Students will learn that there are different types of soil and that all soil is made up of a mixture of ingredients.

Get a Load of This!

Here's a chance for your students to dig into the topic of soil—literally! In advance, scout out locations where students can easily and safely dig in the earth. Before you leave for your destinations, ask children what they think soil is. Guide children to summarize that soil is another name for dirt. Then give each child a small Ziploc bag and digging tools, such as a craft stick and a spoon. Escort youngsters to the approved digging areas; then invite them to each dig up a bagload of soil. Encourage children to examine their own and each other's bagged soil. Do they look the same?

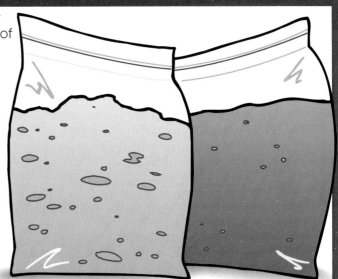

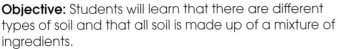

- Mine has stones.
  Jackson

- This one is sparkly.
  Jenna

- I see sand.
  Haley

Check It Out

Upon returning to your classroom, have each child pour his soil onto a different paper plate. Provide magnifying lenses and craft sticks; then encourage children to further examine the soil samples. Do they look the same? Feel the same? Smell the same? What kinds of things are in the soil? Jot children's comments down on a bucket-shaped cutout.

Did You Know...

Soil is made up of a mixture of things, such as small pieces of rock, clay, sand, and decomposing matter like leaves, twigs, and plants.

Sizing Up Soil

This is a spot for plenty of independent exploration! To prepare for this activity, collect several different types of soil, such as potting soil, sand, peat moss, clay, and topsoil. Pour each different type of soil into a different plastic tub or foil pan. (For ease of reference, label each soil sample with a numeral if desired.) Provide spoons, small shovels, magnifying glasses, small sand molds, funnels, and wire strainers. Encourage children to use the supplies to explore each different soil sample. Prompt youngsters to ask themselves questions such as these:

- Which soil is the softest?
- How does each soil smell?
- Which soils can be molded? Which ones fall apart?
- Which soils will go through a funnel?
- Which soils can be sifted through the wire strainer?

After the soils have been thoroughly explored, add a water-filled plant sprayer or watering can to the supplies and invite children to engage in some marvelously muddy free exploration.

Weighing In

Does each type of soil weigh the same? Let's see!

Materials needed:

copy of the reporting sheet on page 103 for each child
2 different types of soil
2 identical measuring cups

balance scale
counters (such as small blocks)
glue
crayons or pencils

Arrange the supplies listed above in your science center. When a child visits the center, have him spread a thin coat of glue on the top left tray on the reporting sheet. Instruct him to sprinkle one type of soil on the glue. Next, have him fill a measuring cup with that type of soil and place it on the scale. Then have him place the empty measuring cup on the other side and fill it with counters until the scale is balanced. Instruct the child to draw (or write) the number of counters needed on the reporting sheet. Have each child repeat this activity, using the other type of soil. To extend this activity, weigh a variety of soil samples, duplicating the reporting sheet as needed. Staple each child's pages together and encourage him to take his report home to share with his family.

Wet or Dry

Now that your young scientists have practiced weighing soil samples, ask them what they think will happen if they weigh the same type of soil dry and then wet. Then encourage them to find out! For each child, duplicate the reporting sheet on page 103. Have the child glue the same type of soil to each of the cups on the left sides of the scales. Then direct the child to write "dry" or "wet," respectively, above each soil sample. Have each child pour some dry soil into a container; then instruct her to weigh the soil using counters. Have her record the weight on the reporting sheet. Next, have the child add some water to the soil and stir it. Then have her weigh the soil. What happened?

Did You Know...

There are pockets of air in soil. When water is added to the soil, it fills up those air pockets, making the wet soil weigh more.

...7, 8, 9...

Just Drainin' Through

Explore the drainage properties of various soils with this fascinating activity. In advance, collect three same-sized flowerpots with drainage holes in the bottoms. Fill each pot with a different type of soil. Arrange each pot over a drainage tray. While one student slowly pours a cup of water into one of the pots, have the rest of the class steadily clap and count aloud until they spy water dripping from the bottom of the pot. Record the number of claps. Then repeat this process using the other pots and soils. Which one drained through the fastest? Do you know why?

This Is Why

Each type of soil contains a different number of air pockets. The water drains through the air pockets. So the more air pockets there are in the soil, the faster the water drains through it.

Name _____

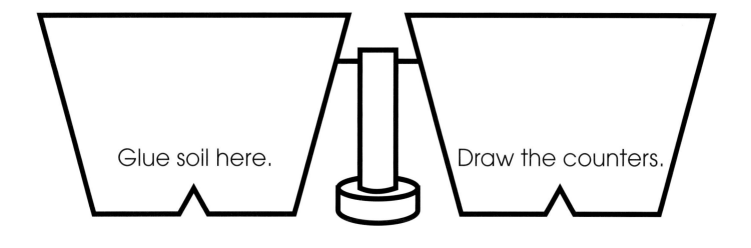

Glue soil here.   Draw the counters.

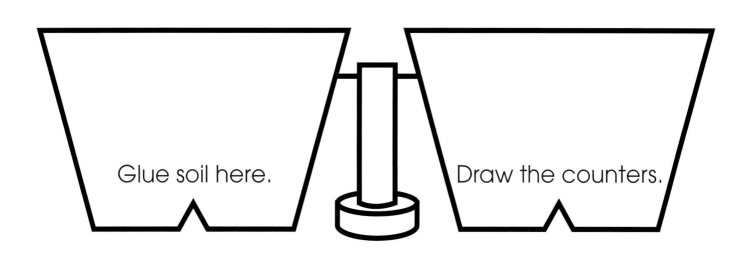

Glue soil here.   Draw the counters.

Explorations

The Root of the Matter

Communicating. Observing. Predicting. A variety of science-process skills will sprout up with this experiment involving a favorite edible root—the carrot!

STEP 1

Yes	No
James	Emily
Sue	Jake
Bob	David
Jamie	Tyrell
Nader	
Kathy	

Cut out a carrot-shaped chart from bulletin board paper; then label it as shown. Show your youngsters the carrots and ask them, "Do you think we can get these carrots to grow?" Discuss and then record each child's response on the chart.

STEP 2

Show students a carrot and explain that the orange part is the *root* and grows under the ground. Then show students the spot on the carrot where the leaves begin to grow. Explain that this is called the *growing tip*. Pass the carrots around for your youngsters to examine.

STEP 5

Fill the pie pans with sand; then push the carrot tops into the sand. Wet the sand thoroughly. Have students predict what they think will happen to the tops.

STEP 6

Check on the carrots each day and water the sand to keep it wet. In less than a week, new leaves will begin to sprout out of the carrot tops!

Science You Can Do
by Suzanne Moore

To investigate carrots, you will need the following:
bunch of carrots with the greens still attached
knife (for teacher use only)
cutting board
foil pie pans
sand
container of water

Cut off the leaves of each carrot without cutting into the growing tip.

Cut off the bottoms of each carrot. Be sure to leave one inch below the growing tip.

This Is Why

Each carrot top contains almost everything the plant needs to grow. The root contains food for the plant, but the plant also needs water. Watering the root helps the carrot top receive the food and begin producing more leaves.

What Now?

Your youngsters have observed carrots sprouting. Now invite them to enjoy this edible root dipped in this delicious dip!

In-the-Pink Dip

Ingredients:
8 oz. soft cream cheese
⅔ c. sour cream
5 tbsp. tomato juice
2 tbsp. dry Italian salad dressing mix

Thoroughly mix the ingredients in a large mixing bowl. Serve immediately with carrot sticks or baby carrots.

Wonders Never Cease

Send In the Clouds

Whether they are rolling, drifting, or billowing across the sky, there are almost always visible clouds that beckon little ones to look up in wonder. Use these ideas to help your youngsters get their heads *and* hands into the clouds.

ideas contributed by Dr. Suzanne Moore

Objective: Students will observe clouds and cloud movements, create cloud art, and learn that clouds are formed when warm air meets cooler air.

Key In on Clouds

Choose a day full of clouds to acquaint your students with these billowy bundles. Load up on blankets or towels and a supply of clipboards and chalk; then head outside for some curious cloud watching. (To make kiddie clipboards, see the illustration.) As youngsters observe the clouds, prompt them to draw what they see. Encourage them to share their observations, using lots of descriptive vocabulary. When you return to the classroom, review each child's comments, recording them on a cloud-shaped cutout. Then display the children's drawings around that cloud.

rubber bands

sturdy cardboard

blue paper

- white
- grey
- fluffy
- puffy
- cotton candy
- soft
- yellow
- like feathers
- ice creamy

Cloud Gazing

Artfully explore clouds further with an activity that will leave a pleasant reminder on your classroom windows or walls. Delight students and inspire cloudy visions by reading aloud Eric Carle's *Little Cloud.* After sharing the book, invite each child to use blue and white tempera paints to paint his own original cloud formations. When the paint is dry, have each child cut out his cloudy picture. Display these pictures and students' dictations around your classroom near the caption shown.

Hands in the Clouds

After your class cloud-watching experience, increase each child's awareness of different types of clouds by sharing *The Cloud Book* by Tomie dePaola. (Although the text is lengthy in places, you'll find it easy to paraphrase or just share parts of the book.) Also display pictures from *The Weather Sky* by Bruce McMillan. Afterward, clear off some tabletops and get ready for some hands-on cloud sculpting. Squirt out a large handful of shaving cream in each child's workspace. Invite her to sculpt any kind of cloud. (A child can use her hands or the back of a spoon to do the sculpting.) As youngsters design and redesign various types of clouds, prompt them to use some of the cloud vocabulary from the book. To clean up, simply have each child wipe off her workspace with a damp paper towel or sponge.

Today we watched the clouds float by and saw these shapes up in the sky.

It looks like a bear to me. Jason

Somebody's shoe... like a big giant! Sally

They could be white crayons. Jess

Clouds on the Move

Set up a center to make these cloud books, designed to reveal the fact that clouds are always on the move! For each child, make a copy of page 108 and several copies of page 109. Also tape a tagboard frame on a classroom window through which clouds can be seen. Staple each title page to several copies of the book page. Encourage each child to visit this center several times—one time for each page in his book.

During the first visit, have each child write her name and color the title page. Then have her write the number of the observation on the second page. Next, encourage the child to look through the frame on the window and observe the clouds within that space. Instruct her to illustrate what she sees on her page. At different times during the day or week, have each child complete each remaining page in a similar manner. Discuss the completed books during a group time, guiding children to determine that clouds are always on the move. Can they guess what makes the clouds move?

Clouds on the Move

by

Maggie

Observation Number ___1___

Concocting Clouds

Present the following scenarios to your clever little cloud makers:

- Stand very close to a mirror—so close that you can breathe on it. What happens?

- Have you ever seen your breath in front of you on a cold day? Then you actually saw a little cloud!

Did You Know...

The little clouds that you make with your breath are like the clouds in the sky. They are formed when warm, moist air hits cooler air.

Clouds on the Move

by

Observation Number _____

Backyard Science: The Five Senses

Any little one who's ever spent time in a backyard or park has had many sense-filled experiences! Use your youngsters' ready-made outdoor expertise to help them focus on this scientific study of the five senses.

ideas by Lucia Kemp Henry

Sights to See

Start this five-senses study by polling your sharp-eyed students about the plants and animals they've spotted in a backyard or park. In advance, cut the tops of two 12" x 18" sheets of white construction paper into zigzags to make two picket fence posters. To make grass, fringe-cut two 2" x 18" strips of green construction paper and then staple one strip to the bottom of each poster. Label one poster "Backyard Plants" and the other one "Backyard Animals." Next, to inspire students' thoughts, share a backyard-related book, such as *Feathers for Lunch* by Lois Ehlert. Then have youngsters brainstorm a list of plants and a list of animals that can be seen in a backyard. Write student suggestions on the appropriate poster, and add to the lists as your five-senses study progresses.

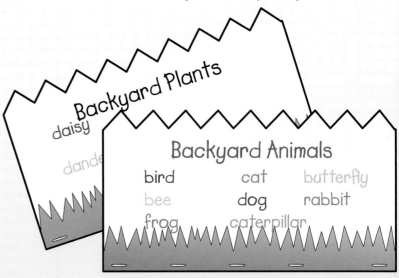

Backyard Plants
daisy
dande[lion]

Backyard Animals
bird   cat   butterfly
bee   dog   rabbit
frog   caterpillar

I Feel A...

Get in touch with your youngsters' scientific curiosity with this easy activity. To prepare, gather a supply of small backyard objects, such as a leaf, a rock, a twig, blades of grass, a snail shell, a short garden hose, a seed packet, and a ball. Place all of the items in a container under a table. Invite two children to the table. Have one youngster sit in a chair and the other one sit next to the container under the table. Instruct the child under the table to hand her partner one of the objects. Direct the youngster to hold the object under the table and explore it with her sense of touch. Encourage her to ask her partner yes-or-no questions to help identify the object. Have the child guess the object's identity. Then invite her to remove the item from under the table and check her guess. Play continues until all of the items in the container have been explored; then the youngsters switch roles. I feel a rock!

Sharpening Our Sight

Help students sharpen their sense of sight with this camouflage experiment. In advance, cut a supply of small butterfly shapes from primarily green samples of wallpaper. (This will give you green butterflies if the printed side shows and white butterflies if the back side shows.) Next, fill your sensory table with green Easter grass or shredded green bulletin board paper to simulate a grassy lawn. Place the butterflies in the faux grass, making sure some green sides face up and some white sides face up. Invite a small group of students to the table. Explain that some animals' bodies cannot be easily seen in their environment. This is called *camouflage*. Then have the children search for the butterflies in the grass. Each time a youngster finds a butterfly, have him pick it up and say the color of butterfly that he has found. As the children call out colors, keep a tally on a sheet of paper. After a minute or so, count the tally marks for each color of butterfly and then discuss the results with the children. Lead students to conclude that no matter how sharp their sense of sight, it's more difficult to see butterflies that are camouflaged. "Green!"

Exploring Backyard Textures

Want your young researchers to get a real "feel" for science exploration? Then invite each child to investigate the outdoors and record various textures by making one of these unique rubbings. Provide each child with a 12" x 18" sheet of white paper and a crayon; then head outdoors.

Have each student explore the various textures on the playground. Encourage her to place her paper over each interesting texture she finds and then use her crayon to make a rubbing of it. Display the finished projects on a bulletin board titled "Backyard Textures."

The flower looks ruffled and pink. It feels smooth and cool. It smells like spices.

Take Time to Sense the Flowers

Smell, sight, and touch will be the senses your students use with this blooming activity. In advance, purchase several different flowers. Divide students into small groups, and give each one a different flower. Have the group explore its flower using the senses of sight, touch, and smell. Then give each child a sheet of white paper and have him draw and color a picture of the flower that he has studied. Next, ask each group to describe how its flower looks, feels, and smells. Write student descriptions in the center of a sheet of chart paper. Help the group glue its drawings around the edge of the chart to create a floral border. Discuss each group's project with the class; then post the charts in a hallway, titling the display "Sensing Flowers."

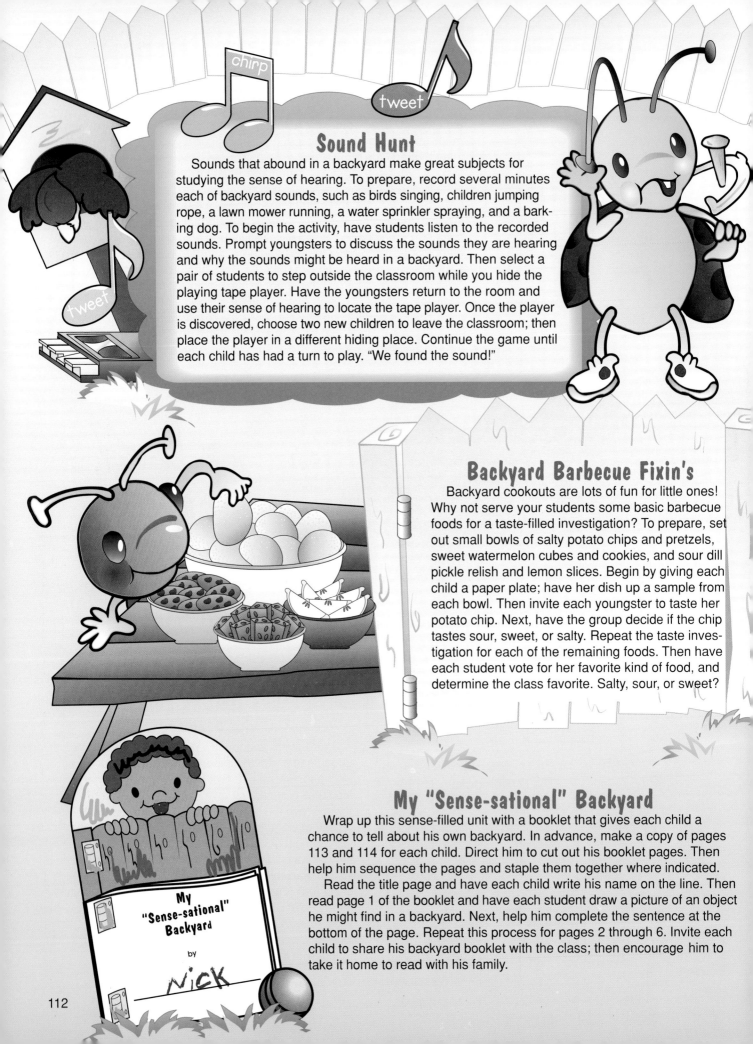

Sound Hunt

Sounds that abound in a backyard make great subjects for studying the sense of hearing. To prepare, record several minutes each of backyard sounds, such as birds singing, children jumping rope, a lawn mower running, a water sprinkler spraying, and a barking dog. To begin the activity, have students listen to the recorded sounds. Prompt youngsters to discuss the sounds they are hearing and why the sounds might be heard in a backyard. Then select a pair of students to step outside the classroom while you hide the playing tape player. Have the youngsters return to the room and use their sense of hearing to locate the tape player. Once the player is discovered, choose two new children to leave the classroom; then place the player in a different hiding place. Continue the game until each child has had a turn to play. "We found the sound!"

Backyard Barbecue Fixin's

Backyard cookouts are lots of fun for little ones! Why not serve your students some basic barbecue foods for a taste-filled investigation? To prepare, set out small bowls of salty potato chips and pretzels, sweet watermelon cubes and cookies, and sour dill pickle relish and lemon slices. Begin by giving each child a paper plate; have her dish up a sample from each bowl. Then invite each youngster to taste her potato chip. Next, have the group decide if the chip tastes sour, sweet, or salty. Repeat the taste investigation for each of the remaining foods. Then have each student vote for her favorite kind of food, and determine the class favorite. Salty, sour, or sweet?

My "Sense-sational" Backyard

Wrap up this sense-filled unit with a booklet that gives each child a chance to tell about his own backyard. In advance, make a copy of pages 113 and 114 for each child. Direct him to cut out his booklet pages. Then help him sequence the pages and staple them together where indicated.

Read the title page and have each child write his name on the line. Then read page 1 of the booklet and have each student draw a picture of an object he might find in a backyard. Next, help him complete the sentence at the bottom of the page. Repeat this process for pages 2 through 6. Invite each child to share his backyard booklet with the class; then encourage him to take it home to read with his family.

My "Sense-sational" Backyard

by

©The Mailbox® • *Science* • TEC1493

What is in the backyard?

I can **see** _____.

1

What is in the backyard?
I can **see** it, **hear** it, **smell** it, **touch** it, or **taste** it!

It is _____.

Staple pages here.

9

Booklet Pages

Use with "My 'Sense-sational' Backyard" on page 112.

What is in the backyard? I can **touch** _____. 4	What is in the backyard? I can **taste** _____. 5
What is in the backyard? I can **hear** _____. 2	What is in the backyard? I can **smell** _____. 3

Wonders Never Cease
Simple Science for Young Children

Incredible Insects

This introduction to *entomology* (the scientific study of insects) will have your classroom all abuzz about the basics of insects.

ideas contributed by Rhonda Dominguez, Kristin Ganoung, and Lynn Mode

Graphing

Do You Like Bugs?

Find out how many of your youngsters are fond of creepy-crawlies with this handy bug graph. Give each child a 4½" x 6" piece of construction paper. Have him trace his hand on the paper, cut out the pattern, and label it with his name. Then ask the question, "Do you like bugs?" Have each child respond by drawing insects on his cutout if he does or leaving the cutout blank if he does not. Then graph the hands and discuss the results.

Remember to ask the same question at the end of your insect study to see if any of your young entomologists' attitudes have changed.

Observing
Recording

A Buggy Comparison

Use this activity to have students take a closer look at insect parts. In advance, duplicate page 117 on white construction paper for each child. Then draw an insect diagram on construction paper as shown.

To begin the activity, explain to students that *all* insects have three body parts and six legs, and that *most* have wings and two antennae. Then give each youngster a copy of page 117. Instruct her to look for insect characteristics of the animals depicted on her paper. Then have her complete the checklist to determine whether each one is an insect or not. Discuss the results.

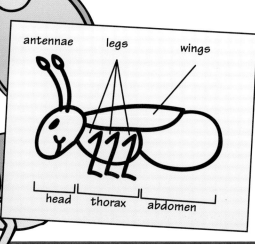

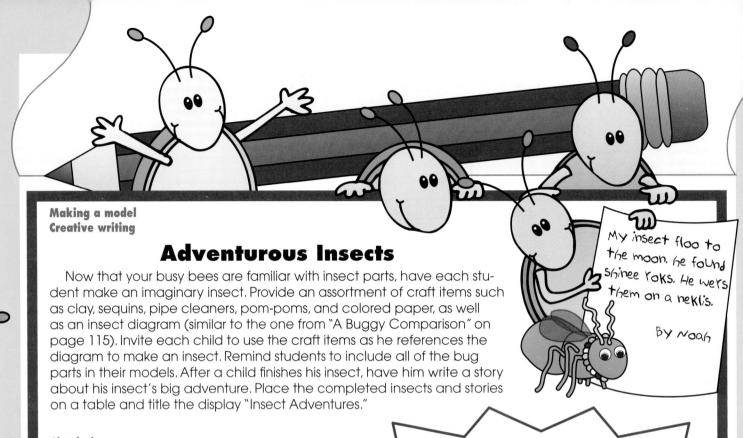

Adventurous Insects

Now that your busy bees are familiar with insect parts, have each student make an imaginary insect. Provide an assortment of craft items such as clay, sequins, pipe cleaners, pom-poms, and colored paper, as well as an insect diagram (similar to the one from "A Buggy Comparison" on page 115). Invite each child to use the craft items as he references the diagram to make an insect. Remind students to include all of the bug parts in their models. After a child finishes his insect, have him write a story about his insect's big adventure. Place the completed insects and stories on a table and title the display "Insect Adventures."

My insect floo to the moon. he found shinee roks. He wers them on a neklis.

BY Noah

Wiggle Out of That Skeleton!

Give your students a lesson in molting with this simulation activity. Prepare an insect "body" by putting a gallon-size storage bag inside a quart-size one. Then place the two bags inside a sandwich bag, aligning the bags' openings. Shred enough green paper to stuff a gallon-size storage bag.

Explain the molting process to your students (see above). Tell them that the three bags represent a growing bug. Hold the bug while several children feed it shredded paper, making sure the paper is being placed inside the largest innermost bag. As the sandwich bag becomes stuffed, explain that the insect needs to molt in order to grow more. Have a child grasp the outer bag and pull it away from the other two bags. Now the insect has a new outer covering and there is room to get bigger. Continue stuffing paper into the inner bag and repeat the molting process again.

Did You Know?

An insect has a skeleton on the outside of its body. It's called an *exoskeleton*. This hard covering protects the insect from drying out and gives the animal its shape. As the insect gets bigger, it outgrows this covering. The exoskeleton splits to let the insect wiggle out. This is called *molting*. A new, bigger exoskeleton dries and hardens on the insect's exterior.

On the Move

Your students are sure to crawl right into this insect movement game. Cut out pictures of crawling, flying, or hopping insects from magazines and glue each of them on a separate index card. Give one card to each child and have her determine how the insect moves. Next, instruct each student to move around the room like her insect would. While she is moving, have each youngster look for other children moving in the same manner and group herself with them. Once the groups are formed, have each child share her insect card with the other group members. Ready, set, move!

Name_____

A Buggy Comparison

Look at each animal.
Complete the checklist.

	must have 3 body parts ✓	must have 6 legs ✓	Is it an insect? Yes = ☺ No = ☹

Down at the Pond

What's happening down at the pond? Plenty! Use this multidisciplinary unit to discover the natural wonders of animal life at the pond.

ideas by Lucia Kemp Henry and Mackie Rhodes

"Pond-erables"

To get things started, arrange a well-supervised trip to a pond that offers lots of hands-on experiences to ponder. Encourage students to identify, photograph, and observe as many different animals as they can. If a trip to a pond is not possible, use a resource book such as *Eyewitness: Pond & River* by Steve Parker to introduce students to various pond animals. Extend your introduction by inviting resource personnel—such as a naturalist, a park ranger, or a Cooperative Extension agent—to bring in some common pond dwellers. Youngsters will find pond life fascinating—naturally!

A Pond With a View

Ever wonder what it's like to be right on a pond? Give youngsters a duck's-eye view of a pond with Nancy Tafuri's *Have You Seen My Duckling?* As you share this story, ask students to search each illustration to find the many different pond inhabitants. Then write a child-generated list of pond animals on chart paper. After they name as many animals as they can remember from the book, have youngsters brainstorm other pond dwellers. Then invite a few students at a time to illustrate some of the listed animals in the margins and open spaces on the paper. What a view!

ducks
fish
frog
beaver
turtle
birds
snail

Pond Pizzazz

Create a dazzling pond display with these specialized fingerpaintings. Have each child create a pond-water effect by swirling blue and green fingerpaints on fingerpaint paper. Invite her to sprinkle iridescent glitter or salt over her wet painting. Then arrange the dry, sparkly paintings on a bulletin board—overlapping the edges—to resemble a pond. Encourage children to decorate the area surrounding the pond with various plant cutouts. Use this pond display as a background for "Pond Spies." The result? A pond with pizzazz!

Pond Spies

This daily pond-inspection center will keep youngsters "ac-count-able" for their visual skills and counting practice. To prepare, make a class supply of an open graph. Also make a supply of the animal patterns on page 122. Color, cut out, and laminate each pattern. Each day, choose a small group of students to pin a desired number of each animal to the pond scene created in "Pond Pizzazz." Have students count and then graph the number of each animal type. If desired, enlarge the graph and do this activity as a whole-group project. "Today at the pond, I spy…."

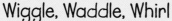

Wiggle, Waddle, Whirl

Youngsters will discover that movement is a way of life down at the pond when you share *In the Small, Small Pond* by Denise Fleming. In advance, convert your water table into a simulated pond. Then gather an assortment of waterproof craft items—such as small plastic lids, sheets of craft foam, foam trays, egg cups, and packing pieces. Also provide pipe cleaners, fabric paints, and waterproof glue. After sharing the story, discuss the different pond animals and their movements. Then invite each child to create his own pond creature using the provided materials. Have him experiment, moving his creature in various ways in your pond. Then invite each child to snap a photo or draw a picture of his creature. Mount each picture on paper; then have the child write/dictate a description of his creature's movements, such as "Wiggle, wobble. Tadpoles are wiggly!" Bind the pages into a class book titled "In Our Small, Small Pond." Share the book, inviting each child to tell about his page.

In Our Small, Small Pond

Wake Up, Pond!

Engage students in some organized "pond-emonium" with this activity. To begin, read aloud *Good Morning, Pond* by Alyssa Satin Capucilli. Then discuss the different sounds and movements that indicate that it's wake-up time at the pond. Invite each child to select an animal to imitate. Have the students group themselves according to where each animal would be found at the pond—*on, around,* or *in* the pond. Have students who select animals that can be found in more than one pond location decide which group they will join. After the groups are formed, call one of the locations—on the pond, in the pond, or around the pond—and have the animals in that group wake up and perform their distinctive movements and noises. When you say, "Good night," have that group go back to its place. Continue in the same manner with the other groups. When you say, "'Pond-emonium,'" *all* the animals will wake up and begin their activities. It's wake-up time at the pond—let the "pond-emonium" begin!

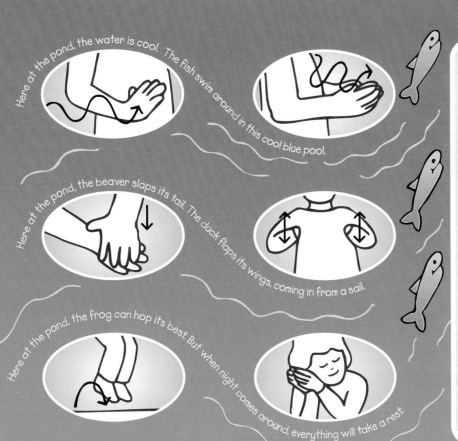

Pond Action Poem

Use this poem and the corresponding motions to get students into reading, science, oral language, and movement. First, write the poem on a sheet of chart paper. After you've introduced the poem to your students, put it in your art area during center time. Encourage children to drop by and contribute to illustrating the page.

Here at the pond,
The water is cool.
The fish swim around
In this cool, blue pool.

Here at the pond,
The beaver slaps its tail.
The duck flaps its wings,
Coming in from a sail.

Here at the pond,
The frog can hop its best.
But when night comes around,
Everything will take a rest.

My Little Pond Book

Here's a book for little ones to prepare and ponder. For each child, duplicate pages 122–124. Have each child cut out his animal patterns, cover, and pages. Help the child read each page and name the pictured animals. Have him complete each page by gluing each animal in the appropriate space and writing the correct numeral in the box. Then have him sequence the pages behind the cover and staple the book along the left edge. Invite him to color each page as he likes. Then encourage youngsters to take their books home to share with their families.

Paper Plate Pond Craft

These 3-D pond crafts are fun to make and impressive to look at. To make one, you will need a thin white paper plate, green construction paper scraps, blue and green tempera paint, paintbrushes, crayons, scissors, glue, and a stapler. (Optional materials: sand, pipe cleaners, small sticks or twigs, and the pond animal patterns from page 122.)

1. Cut the plate so that one section is approximately one inch wider than the other. Color the top portion of the front side of the wider piece brown. (Or, if desired, apply glue to that portion and sprinkle on sand. When the glue is dry, shake off the excess sand; then glue on pieces of twigs or sticks.)

2. Cut green paper scraps to resemble pond plant life. Glue these cutouts to the colored plate. Also add pipe cleaner accents if desired.

3. Paint the back side of the smaller plate piece with blue/green tempera paint. When the paint dries, staple the painted piece to the larger piece as shown.

4. Use art supplies to make pond animals. Or duplicate, color, and cut out the animal patterns from page 122. Glue the animals to the scene as you like.

Display each child's finished project on a board titled "Down at the Pond."

Animal Patterns
Use with "Pond Spies" on page 119 and "My Little Pond Book" and "Paper Plate Pond Craft" on page 121.

Book Cover
Use with "My Little Pond Book" on page 121.

The Pond

by _____

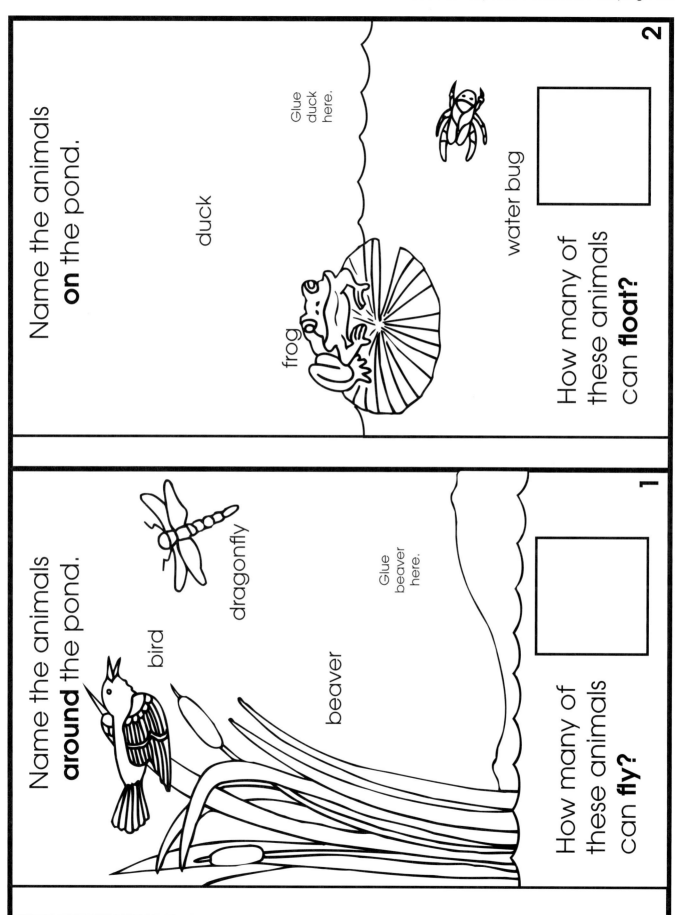

2

Name the animals **on** the pond.

duck

Glue duck here.

frog

water bug

How many of these animals can **float?**

1

Name the animals **around** the pond.

dragonfly

bird

beaver

Glue beaver here.

How many of these animals can **fly?**

Book Pages

Use with "My Little Pond Book" on page 121.

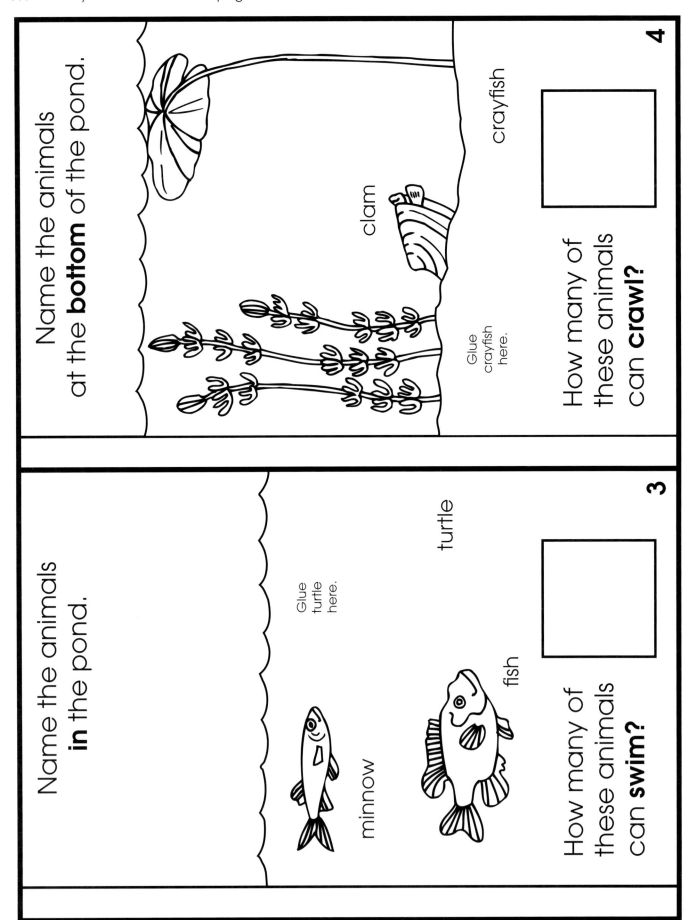

Name the animals at the **bottom** of the pond.

crayfish

clam

Glue crayfish here.

How many of these animals can **crawl?**

4

Name the animals **in** the pond.

turtle

Glue turtle here.

fish

minnow

How many of these animals can **swim?**

3

Seashell Sensations

Dive into observation skills with these super seashell activities.

ideas by Suzanne Moore

The Shape of Shells

Start your seashell study with a small-group activity that is cloaked in mystery. Before students arrive for the day, scatter several shells on the floor and then cover them with a large beach towel. Invite a small group of students to the area and explain that you have hidden mystery objects under the towel. Invite each child to feel one of the objects through the towel. Encourage students to describe what they feel and then guess what is under the towel. After each child has made a guess, remove the towel to reveal the shells. Have students closely examine the shells and then discuss their observations.

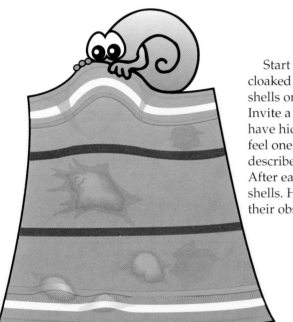

DID YOU KNOW?
Every seashell was once the home of a sea animal.

Shell Centers

Continue to sharpen students' observation skills with these easy-to-create centers.

- Stock an area with a basket of small shells and several copies of the sorting sheet on page 126. Direct students to sort the shells onto the sheet by appearance.
- Place several shells near a supply of play dough and invite each child to make impressions of the shells in the dough.
- Stock an area with a supply of shells, hand lenses, paper, and crayons. Encourage each child to use the lenses to closely examine the shells. Then direct her to use the crayons and paper to trace the shells and make rubbings.
- Place some shells near a balance scale and a supply of counting blocks. Invite students to use the scale and blocks to weigh the shells.

Read aloud *What Lives in a Shell?* by Kathleen Weidner Zoehfeld.

Name _____

Shell Sorting

Note to the teacher: Use with "Shell Centers" on page 125.

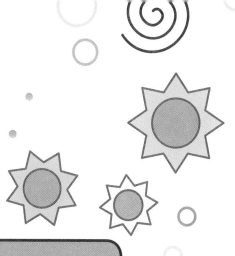

Anytime Science

Wonders Never Cease
Simple Science for Young Children

A Bounty of Bubbles

This introduction to "bubble-ology" (the scientific study of bubbles, of course!) will have your classroom bursting with discoveries all about the basics of bubbles.

ideas by Dr. Suzanne Moore

Objective: Students will learn that bubbles are made up of air that is surrounded by a thin liquid skin. They will also discover that bubbles can only be made through objects that have holes in them.

Bubble Brew

When you make the bubble recipe to the right, be sure to use bottled water. (Some tap water contains minerals that make bubble blowing more difficult.) Let this solution sit for about five days before you use it. The longer the bubble mixture ages, the better the bubbles! Why not mix up a big batch of Bubble Brew at the beginning of school to use throughout the year?

Basic Bubble Brew
Gently stir together the following:
1 gallon of water
⅔ cup Dawn dishwashing liquid
1 tbsp. glycerin

Bubbling Over

This air-filled activity prompts youngsters to use their observing and predicting skills—but it might leave them just a little bit breathless!

Materials needed:
paper cup for each child
plastic straw for each child
water

Dawn dishwashing liquid
paper towels for cleanup

After filling each cup halfway with water, give each child a cup and a straw. Invite children to use their straws to blow bubbles in the water. Ask youngsters why they think the bubbles were made. Then add two to three drops of Dawn to each cup. Have each child gently mix the soap and water with her straw. Ask youngsters to predict what will happen when they blow into the soap and water solution. Then have them blow bubbles again. Were there more bubbles this time? Why?

Did You Know...

The outside of a bubble is a very thin film of liquid. Bubbles that are made of soap and water do not break as easily as plain-water bubbles. This is because soapy water sticks together better than plain water.

Note: Any place that bubbles land might become slippery. A vinegar and water solution can be used for easy cleanup.

Blowing Bubbles

This activity gives each child a hands-on opportunity to explore the bubble-making process.

Materials needed:

small paper cup per child   foam bowl for each small group
plastic straw per child   Bubble Brew

In advance, use a sharp pencil to poke a hole about one inch from the bottom of each cup. (The hole should be slightly smaller than the circumference of the straw.) Then pour some Bubble Brew into each bowl. Next, give a cup and a straw to each child. Help each child poke his straw through the hole in his cup. Instruct the child to turn his cup upside down, dip it in the Bubble Brew, and then turn it right side up. What does he see? Have the child gently blow through the straw. What happens? Who knows why? Allow plenty of time for free exploration, encouraging children to try blowing hard, soft, and then not at all.

Did You Know...

Bubbles are filled with air or gas. When you blew into the straw, you filled the bubble with air.

A Rainbow of Colors

Watch in delight as your youngsters discover a wonderful world of color in their bubbles.

Materials needed:
bubble pipes made in "Blowing Bubbles"

Following the same procedure used in "Blowing Bubbles," have each child blow a bubble with her back to the sunlight. Then have her move the bubble so that the sunlight passes through it. What does she see? Why? How many different colors can she identify?

Did You Know...

When the sunlight passes through the bubble, the colors of the rainbow can be seen on the outside of the bubble.

Bubble Catching

Your little scientists will be only too eager to get their hands on this bubbly activity.

Materials needed:
pipe cleaner for each child
several small bowls of Bubble Brew
paper towels for easy cleanup

Begin by showing your students how to bend and twist a pipe cleaner to make a bubble wand. Then group children into pairs. Have one child in each pair blow bubbles while his partner attempts to catch them. Then have the children switch roles and repeat the activity. Prompt children to discuss their discoveries. Then prompt youngsters by saying, "If a bubble breaks when it hits something *dry,* I wonder if it will still break when it hits something…" Then let your youngsters try out their thoughts. (Guide children to try catching bubbles on soapy fingers, straws, and bubble blowers. You can even have one child blow a bubble while another child sticks a soapy straw right into it!)

Did You Know...

A bubble's thin skin is made of liquid. When it lands on something dry, the liquid is absorbed by the dry object and the bubble pops. When a bubble comes in contact with a wet surface, the wet surface simply becomes part of the bubble.

Bubbles or Bust

Exactly what kinds of things can be used to make bubbles? In this activity, your students will be judges of that. Provide a supply of objects that children can immerse in bubble solution. (Be sure that you have a mixture of objects with and objects without holes, such as a pair of scissors, a plastic berry basket, a spoon, and a ruler.) Place the objects in a center, along with a large bowl of Bubble Brew and a copy of the recording sheet (on page 131) for each child. When a child visits this center, have her choose one of the objects and write it (or draw it) on her recording sheet. Then have her indicate her prediction by drawing a happy face (for yes) if bubbles can be made or a sad face (for no) if bubbles can't be made. Next, have her test it out and record the results. Extend this activity by asking children to bring in additional items to try out in this bubble-making center. Did you get bountiful bubbles, or was it a bust?

Some other bubble-making props:

mason jar lids	flyswatters	colanders
slotted spatulas	whisks	plastic bangle bracelets
cookie cutters	plastic six-pack rings	

Name ___Sarah___

Can it make bubbles?

Object	Prediction	Result

Name _____

 Can it make bubbles?

Object	Prediction	Result

Note to the teacher: Use with "Bubbles or Bust" on page 130.

Explorations

Two "Sound" Ideas!

It only takes a few simple materials to explore the science of sound. How do you like the sound of that?

STEP 1

Give each child in a small group a wooden paint stick to examine. Have students brainstorm ways to make the stick move and make noise.

STEP 2

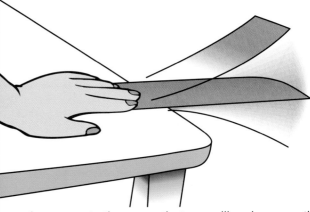

Announce to the group that you will make your stick move and make noise. Extend the stick over the edge of a table. Firmly hold one end of the stick onto the table and then pluck the other end. Have students observe and listen carefully.

STEP 5

Help each child use a rubber band to wrap a square of waxed paper tightly around the unpunched end of the tube.

STEP 6

Have each child hold the open end of the tube to his mouth and sing loudly into the tube. Guide the child to notice the vibrations in the tube as he sings.

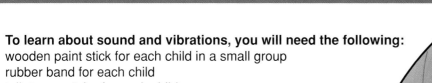

Science You Can Do *by Suzanne Moore*

To learn about sound and vibrations, you will need the following:
wooden paint stick for each child in a small group
rubber band for each child
toilet paper tube for each child
5" x 5" square of waxed paper for each child
hole puncher

STEP 3

Invite each child to hold her stick on the table and pluck the end. Have the child create different sounds by varying the length that extends beyond the table. Or have the child pluck the stick and then slide it while it is in motion. Allow students plenty of time for exploration and then discuss their observations.

STEP 4

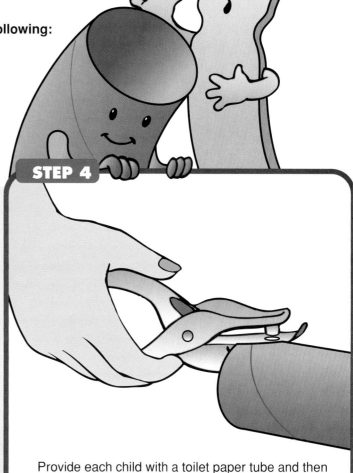

Provide each child with a toilet paper tube and then punch a hole in one end of the tube.

This Is Why

- All sound is caused by movement or *vibrations.*
- The plucked paint stick quickly moved back and forth, or *vibrated.*
- Different sizes of vibrating objects can create different sounds. When the length of the extended paint stick changed, the sound also changed.
- Singing into the toilet paper tube caused the waxed paper to vibrate and create a sound.

What Now?

- Repeat the first activity using other objects, such as a plastic ruler, plastic spoon, or rubber spatula.
- Cover the hole in the toilet paper tube while singing into it. Does it make a different sound? Try it and see!

133

Explorations

Pulling Power

Little ones will be attracted to this series of simple experiments involving magnets.

STEP 1

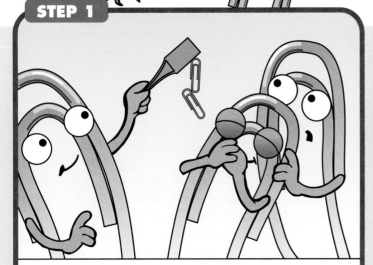

Show each child in a small group a magnet and the paper clips. Allow the students to explore the magnets and clips. Then have students discuss their observations.

STEP 2

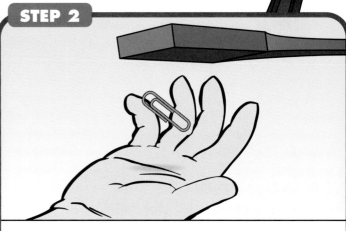

Have a child hold a paper clip in the palm of his hand. Then direct him to hold a magnet in his other hand and slowly lower it toward the clip. Instruct the group to observe the paper clip closely. When the magnet gets close enough to the clip, the clip will "jump" out of the child's hand and stick to the magnet!

STEP 5

Provide the group with a small paper cup. Have a child place a paper clip inside the cup. Then direct him to touch the outside of the cup with the magnet as the group observes the movement of the clip.

STEP 6

Cover the paper clip in the cup with a small amount of dry rice. Then have a child hold the magnet over the rice. The paper clip will jump up and stick to the magnet, leaving the rice inside the cup. Collect the materials for the next small group.

Science You Can Do *by Suzanne Moore*

To explore magnets, you will need the following:
strong magnetic wand
1" newspaper square
large paper clips
paper cup for each small group
dry rice

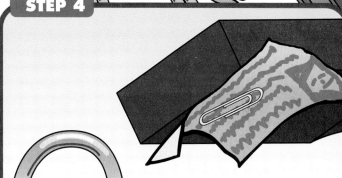

STEP 3

Set the paper clips aside. Provide the group with a small newspaper square. Direct a child to repeat Step 2 using the newspaper instead of a paper clip. Have the group compare the results. *(The newspaper will not jump or stick to the magnet.)*

STEP 4

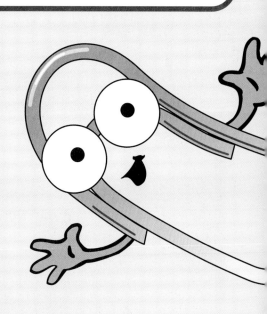

Direct a child to place a paper clip in the palm of his hand and then cover it with the newspaper square. Have the child repeat Step 2 using the newspaper and the clip. The clip will jump to the magnet and carry the newspaper with it!

This Is Why

- Only objects containing iron are attracted to magnets.
- Paper clips are made of a metal that contains iron.
- The magnetic force can act through some surfaces, such as the newspaper square, the side of the cup, and the rice.

C'mon, Everybody, Let's Rock!

Did you know that everybody lives on a rock? That's because rocks cover the whole earth! Use the ideas in this unit to get students exploring this form of matter that is all around us. C'mon, everybody!

ideas by Susan A. DeRiso and Lynn C. Mode

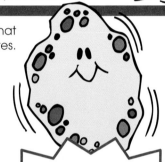

Objective: Students will use scientific-process skills to explore rocks. Students will learn that rocks come in many different shapes and sizes and possess various observable attributes.

Safety: Safety goggles should be worn during all activities in which there is any potential for liquids or solids to accidentally get into the eyes.

Collecting data

Getting Ready for Rocks

Enlist the help of your little rock hounds to gather the main ingredients of this unit! Give each child a paper lunch bag to take home. Ask him to search for an assortment of different rocks. Encourage children to look in places such as their backyards, schoolyards, parks, or even gardening shops (with permission). Have each child bring his bag of rocks back to school and you're ready to rock on!

Did You Know?
People collect all sorts of different things. But rocks are the *oldest* things a person can collect!

Did You Know?
A person who studies rocks is called a *petrologist.* Gee! Maybe that's for me!

Observing Communicating Defining

Discovery!

Please do not disturb—young petrologists are hard at work in this discovery center! To prepare the center, provide a tub of water, a few toothbrushes, paper towels, and a pencil. (Also have a sheet of chart paper and a marker nearby for you.) When a child visits this center, have her write her name on a paper towel. Then invite her to dip her rocks in the water, scrub them with a toothbrush, and put them on her labeled towel. As children verbalize their discoveries, write them on the chart paper. What wonderful rock discoveries!

Observing Communicating Defining

Can We Talk?

Youngsters will uncover vocabulary galore in just a little conversation about rocks! After each child has had a chance to clean and study his rocks (in "Discovery!"), gather your students in view of the rocks and the chart that you started during that activity. Review the words already on the chart. Then invite students to look at and handle the dry rocks. Encourage children to describe what they notice; then record their responses on the chart, adding picture cues as desired. Wow—that's a load of language!

shiny	square
not shiny	oval
small	striped
bumpy	scratchy
speckled	round

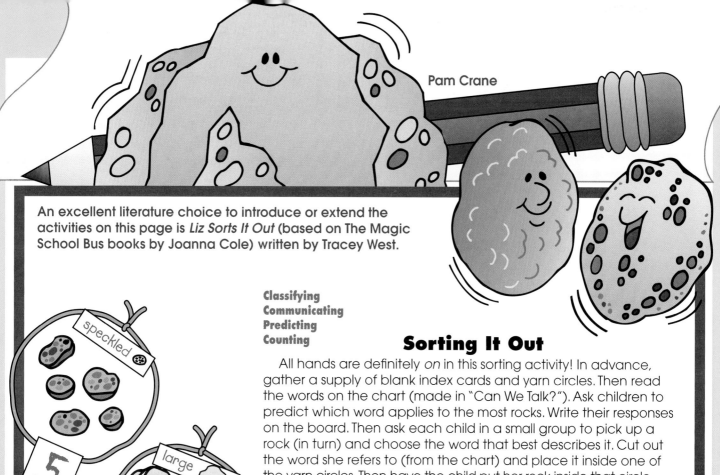

Pam Crane

An excellent literature choice to introduce or extend the activities on this page is *Liz Sorts It Out* (based on The Magic School Bus books by Joanna Cole) written by Tracey West.

Classifying
Communicating
Predicting
Counting

Sorting It Out

All hands are definitely *on* in this sorting activity! In advance, gather a supply of blank index cards and yarn circles. Then read the words on the chart (made in "Can We Talk?"). Ask children to predict which word applies to the most rocks. Write their responses on the board. Then ask each child in a small group to pick up a rock (in turn) and choose the word that best describes it. Cut out the word she refers to (from the chart) and place it inside one of the yarn circles. Then have the child put her rock inside that circle. Repeat the process until all the rocks have been sorted. Ask different children to count the rocks in the circles and record the numbers on index cards. Place each number card near its corresponding circle. Discuss the results. (Don't dismantle the sorted collection just yet! You'll need it for "Same *and* Different.")

Classifying
Justifying decisions

Same *and* Different

Securely fasten all thinking caps for this mind-expanding activity! Refer your students to the sorting circles from "Sorting It Out." Ask children if any of the rocks could go in more than one circle. For example, is there a *small* rock that is also *bumpy*? If so, show students how to overlap the edges of the two circles and place the rock in the middle (as in a Venn diagram). After introducing this activity, keep it available for a science center activity. The possibilities go on and on!

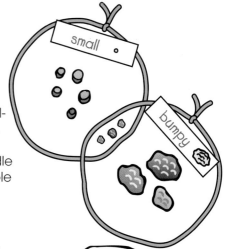

Extension Activities

• Extend the use of the sorted rock collection by making a floor bar graph. Use the labels from the circles to designate each column. The rest is up to the kids!

• For fun and creativity, provide a variety of art supplies and invite each child to decorate one rock to be his pet rock.

• Encourage children to explore the different hardnesses of the rocks by scraping several of them with a penny. Which rocks are harder than a penny? Softer than a penny? Another opportunity for classification!

Literature Links

My Ol' Man by Patricia Polacco
On My Beach There Are Many Pebbles by Leo Lionni

Explorations

Soapy Science

Lather up! This dirt-defying activity will help youngsters understand how soap gets us clean.

STEP 1

Direct a small group of youngsters to wash their hands with water only and then dry their hands with paper towels. Have the students look closely at the towels. Ask, "Do you see any dirt on the towels? Do you think your hands are clean?"

STEP 2

Give each child in the group a small jar half-filled with water. Slowly add one tablespoon of vegetable oil to each jar. Have your students observe the interaction of the oil and the water. Ask, "What happened when oil was added to the water? Where is the water? Where is the oil?"

STEP 5

Have students put the jars on the table again and observe the mixture. Ask, "What happened to the water? What happened to the soap? Where is the oil?"

STEP 6

Have the children wash their hands again, this time using soap. After they dry their hands with paper towels, ask them these questions: "Did you see any dirt being washed away when you washed your hands? Why do you think your hands are really clean this time?"

Science You Can Do
by Suzanne Moore

To discover how soap gets us clean, you will need the following:

paper towels
small, clear plastic jar with a lid for each child
water
tablespoon
tbsp. of vegetable oil for each child
teaspoon
tsp. of liquid dish detergent for each child
soap

STEP 3

Secure the lids on the jars. Then have your students shake their jars for several seconds. Direct the students to put their jars on a table. Again have them observe the oil and water. Ask, "Where is the oil? Where is the water?" Continue watching as the two liquids separate.

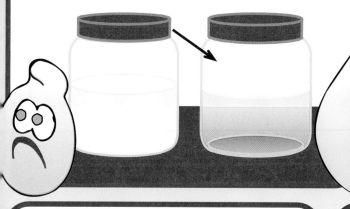

STEP 4

Remove the jar lids; then add one teaspoon of detergent to each jar. Direct your students to watch as the detergent forms its own layer. Secure the lids on the jars; then have students shake their jars again.

This Is Why

- Oil is *insoluble*—it will not dissolve in water.
- When a jar of oil and water is shaken, the oil and water temporarily mix. When the jar is still, the oil and water separate again.
- We get dirty because our skin is slightly oily. Dirt sticks to the oil. When our hands are washed with water only, the oil and dirt do not mix with the water. Therefore our hands stay dirty.
- When oil and water mix, an *emulsion* is formed. Oil is broken into tiny droplets suspended in the water. When soap is used during bathing, it surrounds the dirt and oil so they can be washed away.

What Now?

Copy, color, and cut out this badge for each child. Reward students who remember to wash with soap with a membership into your happy hand-washers club!

Happy Hand Washer

©The Mailbox®

Explorations

Oh, Buoy!
Plunge into some science fun with this investigation of sinking and floating!

STEP 1

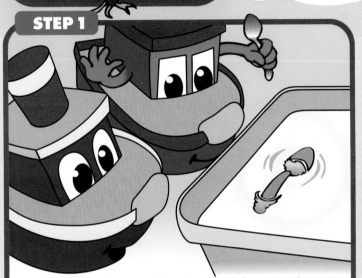

Invite a small group of students to join you at the water table. Illustrate the concept of *sinking* by placing a metal spoon in the water. Then demonstrate *floating* by dropping a plastic spoon in the water.

STEP 2

Have students examine a solid rubber ball and predict whether the ball will sink or float.

STEP 5

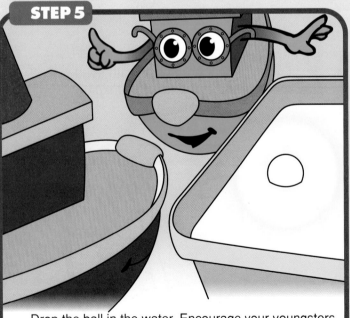

Drop the ball in the water. Encourage your youngsters to observe the ball and then conclude that the ball floats.

STEP 6

Have students examine and compare the two different balls. Invite each child to explain why he thinks one ball floats and one ball sinks.

Science You Can Do

To learn about sinking and floating, you will need the following:
water table or large container filled with water
plastic spoon
metal spoon
solid rubber ball
Ping-Pong ball

STEP 3

Drop the ball in the water. Direct your youngsters to observe the ball; then lead them to conclude that it sinks.

STEP 4

Have students examine a Ping-Pong ball. Discuss the results of Step 3 and then invite youngsters to predict whether the ball will sink or float.

This Is Why

- The plastic spoon and Ping-Pong ball are less dense than the water. Because they are less dense, the water holds them up and they float!
- The metal spoon and rubber ball are more dense than the water. The water cannot hold them up, so they sink.

What Now?

Gather a variety of balls, such as old golf balls, tennis balls, and baseballs. Place the balls near the water table and invite youngsters to predict and then test the buoyancy of each one.

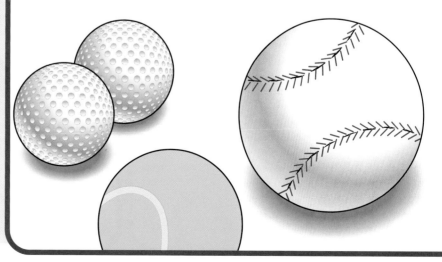

Science

Huff and Puff!

Little ones have a grand time huffing and puffing during this exploration of air!

by Lucia Kemp Henry

Ask a small group of students to sit along one side of a table. Give each child a plastic drinking straw and a craft feather.

Ask each child to move her feather across the table by blowing air through her straw. Ask students why the feathers can be moved in this way. Help them conclude that a craft feather is light and moves easily.

Have students test their predictions.

Have students sort the test objects into three groups according to which ones are easy to move, which ones are hard to move, and which ones can't be moved.

Explorations

To discover whether items can be moved by a stream of air, each student in a small group needs the following:

plastic drinking straw
craft feather
wooden block (or something of similar weight)
cotton ball
small rock
jumbo paper clip
craft stick

STEP 3

Give each child a wooden block. Challenge him to make the block move by blowing air through his straw. Ask students why the block cannot be moved in this way. Help them conclude that a wooden block is heavy and does not move easily.

STEP 4

Give students the remaining objects. Engage them in predicting whether each object can be moved by blowing air through a straw.

This Is Why

When air is forced through a straw, it moves quickly and has strength. The air has the power to move lightweight objects.

What Now?

Invite students to experiment with different ways to move a test object with air. First, suggest that the child try to move the object by blowing air directly on it. Then challenge her to move the object by blowing air through a clean paper towel tube and/or paper cone. Have the student compare the methods and decide which one works best!

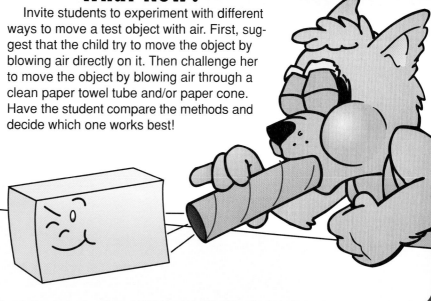

Physical Changes Made Simple

To investigate the magic of physical changes your little ones won't need a special wand or a top hat—just a little powdered drink mix and water.

by Suzanne Moore, Irving, TX

Check It Out

To begin checking out physical changes, help each child in a small group scoop one-fourth teaspoon of powdered drink mix into a personalized clear plastic cup. Encourage your little ones to describe what they see, feel, and smell. Then provide each child with a hand lens and encourage him to take a closer look at the crystals. Emphasize that the powder is a solid.

Presto Change-o!

Delight youngsters with another super simple example of physical change. Ask students what will happen if their drinks are placed in the freezer. How will the drinks change? Pop the cups into the freezer and leave overnight. (Hint: Nestle the drink cups into muffin tins for an easy no-spills trip to the freezer.)

After the drinks are frozen, give each child his cup. Have him examine its contents with a hand lens and describe how his drink looks. Explain that the liquid changed to a solid when it froze. Will the icy snack change again? After youngsters share their thoughts, set the frozen drinks aside. Presto change-o! The frozen treats will melt as they stay at room temperature, and then they'll disappear—when your students drink them!

Abracadabra

Now that your young scientists have investigated the powdered drink mix, pour one-fourth cup of water into each child's cup. Invite him to sing the following song as he stirs his water-powder mixture with a plastic spoon or coffee stirrer until the powder has dissolved into the water. Encourage students to examine their drinks with hand lenses. Ask questions such as these: Can you see any powdered drink mix? Where did it go? How do you know it's still in the water? Explain that the powdered mix only seemed to disappear when it was stirred with water. It actually dissolved. Direct each child to take a small sip of his drink. Lead students to conclude that the mix is still in the water because it has changed colors and it tastes sweet.

(sung to the tune of "Skip to My Lou")

Abracadabra. Stir, stir, stir.
Abracadabra. Stir, stir, stir.
Abracadabra. Stir, stir, stir.
Where did my powdered drink
  mix go?

The Pump That Thumps

What's shaped like an upside-down pear, is hollow, and never rests?
Try these big-hearted activities with students to find out!

by Suzanne Moore, Irving, TX

Heart Basics

Each of your youngsters probably knows she has a heart, but does she know where it's really located and how big it is? Begin your heart study by sharing the following information: The heart is about as big as a person's fist and is located in the center of the chest, tilted slightly to the left. The heart is a pump that pushes blood through vessels throughout the body.

Next, have each child make a fist and place it in the middle of her chest. Then have her pump her fist continuously while singing the song at right. After singing, ask students whether their hands are tired from pumping. Then explain that each of their hearts beats nonstop to pump blood through their bodies all day and all night long.

(sung to the tune of "The Wheels on the Bus")

The heart in my chest goes thump, thump, thump,
Thump, thump, thump,
Thump, thump, thump.
The heart in my chest goes thump, thump, thump
Day and night.

The heart is a pump that pumps my blood,
Pumps my blood, pumps my blood.
The heart is a pump that pumps my blood
Day and night.

Exercise makes it nice and strong,
Nice and strong, nice and strong.
Exercise makes it nice and strong,
Day and night.

DID YOU KNOW?

The average heart beats over 2½ billion times in a lifetime.

Pump It Up

After this simple demonstration, your youngsters will be eager to exercise and then check their pulses. To begin, demonstrate how to feel a pulse along the side of the neck and then have students give it a try. Next, instruct each child to put her head down on her desk and remain still for a couple of minutes. Then have her feel her pulse and note its speed. Next, have students stand up and hop twenty times. Instruct each student to check her pulse again. Then ask, "Is your heart beating faster? Why do you think it changed speed?" After students respond, explain that the speed of a beating heart changes based on the activity level of a person. Way to feel the beat!

The Beat Complete

What can be used to listen to a heart beat? Doctors use stethoscopes to amplify the sounds of the heart. Have youngsters create a similar effect with paper tubes. Pair students and give each twosome a toilet paper tube to share. Quiet the room. Then, in turn, instruct one youngster in each pair to listen to his partner's heartbeat. Next, have students describe the sounds they heard. Explain that the sounds are made by the opening and closing of a heart valve, and by flowing blood.

Explorations

Comparing Parachutes

What goes up must come down! Use this simple experiment to give youngsters a basic introduction to the ups and downs of air resistance and gravity.

STEP 1

Invite a small group of children to join you in making parachutes. Help each child tape a piece of string to each corner of a 14-inch plastic square (as shown).

STEP 2

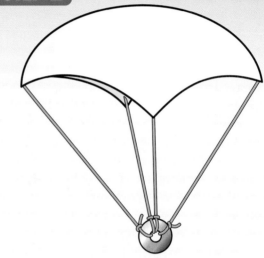

Complete a parachute for each child by tying the loose end of each string to a washer.

STEP 5

Which Will Land First?	
Big	**Little**
John	Kevin
Sarah	Amy
Denise	Beth
Tony	Laura
James	

Have students predict which of the two parachutes will float to the ground first, the large one or the small one. Jot students' predictions on a chart.

STEP 6

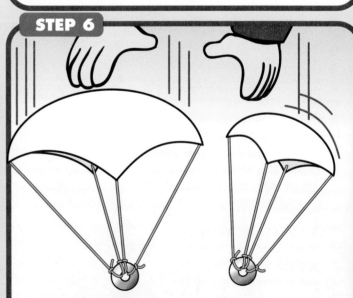

Help each child, in turn, stand on a chair and hold his parachutes in front of him at shoulder height. Then have him drop both parachutes at the same time and watch to see which one lands first.

Science You Can Do *by Suzanne Moore*

To learn about air resistance and gravity, each child will need the following:

eight 16" lengths of string
14" square of plastic, cut from a plastic trash bag
8" square of plastic, cut from a plastic trash bag
masking tape
two ¾" washers

STEP 3

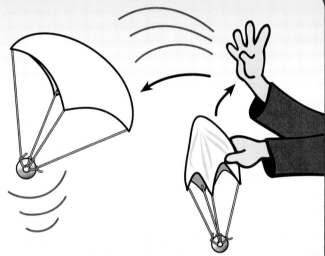

Have each child test his parachute by holding the plastic square, throwing the parachute up in the air, and then watching as it floats to the ground.

STEP 4

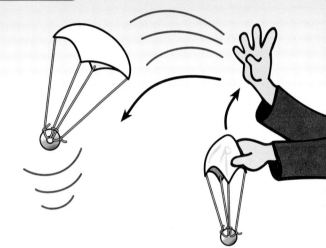

Make a smaller parachute for each child by using an eight-inch plastic square, four strings, some tape, and a washer (see the directions in Step 1 and Step 2). Then have each youngster test the parachute (see Step 3).

This Is Why

- The force of *gravity* pulls the parachutes toward the ground.
- As the parachutes fall, the plastic traps the air.
- The air slows the parachutes down as they fall. This is called *air resistance*.
- The smaller parachute has less *air resistance*—or traps less air—than the bigger parachute, so it falls to the ground first.

What Now?

Make cloth parachutes by threading lengths of string through the corners of handkerchiefs. Tie the loose ends of each string to small lightweight toys, such as plastic figurines. Then set the parachutes in a center for students to explore.

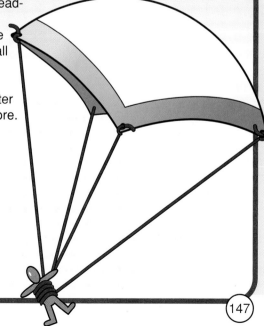

Explorations

Follow the Bouncing Ball

Youngsters' scientific thinking will bounce to new heights with this hot and cold activity!

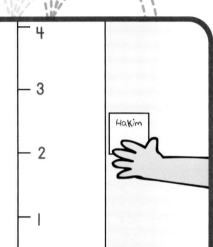

STEP 1

Find an area of your classroom with a blank wall and floor space without carpet. Tape the number line to the wall so that the bottom end touches the floor.

4

3

2

1

STEP 2

Have a small group of students examine the ball. Invite each child to predict how high the ball will bounce. Then have him mark his prediction by placing a personalized sticky note beside the chart.

4

3

2

1

Hakim

STEP 5

The next day, revisit the number line and review the results from the first experiment. Have each child predict how high the frozen ball will bounce; then have him move his sticky note to mark his new prediction.

3

2

1

Hakim

STEP 6

Remove the ball from the freezer and dry it off. Have students briefly examine the frozen ball. Then direct them to carefully observe the ball as you drop it from shoulder height. Record the height of the bounce by taping the labeled ball cutout to the number line. Discuss students' predictions and the results of the experiment.

4

3

2

1

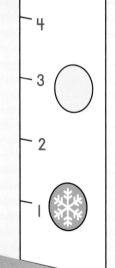

Science You Can Do

To learn how temperature affects the bounce of a ball you will need the following:

solid rubber ball
large vertical number line, such as a growth chart
tape
access to a freezer (or a freezing temperature outside)
pad of sticky notes
two construction paper ball cutouts, one labeled with a
   snowflake stamp or sticker

STEP 3

Hold the ball at shoulder height in front of the number line; then release the ball. Direct students to watch how high the ball bounces on the *first* bounce. (If necessary, drop the ball a few times to give students practice watching the movement of the ball.) Record the height of the bounce by taping the unlabeled ball cutout to the number line.

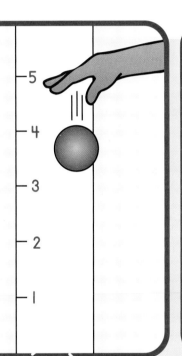

STEP 4

Place the ball in the freezer (or outside) to chill overnight. Then have students predict how the cold will affect the bounce of the ball. Will it bounce higher or lower?

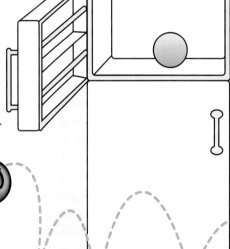

This Is Why

Rubber balls are *elastic.* They stretch out of shape when they are bounced and then quickly return to their original shape. When the ball is chilled in the freezer, the ball loses some of its ability to stretch, or its *elasticity.* A frozen ball will not bounce as high as one at room temperature. If the ball is chilled to an extremely cold temperature it will shatter into tiny pieces instead of bouncing!

What Now?

Do all balls have the same amount of bounce? Invite students to compare the bounce of a baseball, a tennis ball, and a golf ball.

Explorations

Dusting for Prints

This fingerprint investigation is sure to make a mark on little ones' learning!

STEP 1

Give each child in a small group one sheet of paper and a pencil. Help each child trace a hand onto his paper.

STEP 2

Give an index card to each child. Have him repeatedly rub the card with one side of the pencil lead until a layer of graphite forms.

STEP 5

Have the child remove the tape and stick it onto the index finger of his hand outline. Repeat Steps 3–5 to make prints of the child's other fingers.

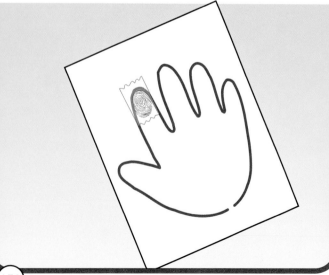

STEP 6

Give each child in the small group a plastic magnifying lens. Have him compare the fingerprints on the tape with the markings on his fingertips. Encourage youngsters to discuss their observations.

Science You Can Do
by Suzanne Moore

To investigate fingerprints, you will need the following:
pencil for each child in a small group
sheet of white paper for each child
small index card for each child
transparent tape
plastic magnifying lenses

STEP 3

Instruct each child to roll the tip of his index finger in the graphite.

STEP 4

Provide each child with a strip of transparent tape. Help him put the tape on the tip of his index finger as shown. Then have him rub the tape so the graphite sticks to it and makes a print.

Did You Know?

- No two people have exactly the same fingerprint.
- Fingerprints are formed five months before birth.

What Now?

Have each child use a black washable ink pad to make a thumbprint on a small piece of paper. Then use a photocopier to enlarge the print. Cut out the enlarged print. Glue it onto a small index card and then label the card with the child's name. Place each child's card at a center and invite youngsters to examine and compare the enlarged prints.

Jeremy

Suna

Animals All Around

Gallop into math, pounce into science, hop into reading and language, and waddle into positive socialization. No matter how you get there, all kinds of learning opportunities are nestled in this thematic unit revolving around all kinds of animals.

Jamie

I like this tiger

Animals
Jamie is
studying tigers.

ideas contributed by Lucia Kemp Henry

Animal Reading Corner

Immerse your youngsters in a wide variety of animals—some familiar and some not so familiar—by stocking your reading center with a collection of animal books (see the list on page 156 for recommended titles). Encourage children to visit the center and carefully examine the animals in the books. Have paper and drawing supplies available for those children who would like to practice writing some of the animal names or who become artistically inspired as they look through the books. During your group times, encourage children to discuss the animals they have been noticing as they read. For continued reference, keep an ongoing record of your youngsters' comments on chart paper.

All Kinds of Animals

Use this poem to reinforce emergent reading skills and oral language, as well as introduce some basic differences and similarities among animals. Copy the poem onto chart paper; then read it aloud to your class. After discussing the poem, read it several times together, having youngsters join in as they are able. When your students are familiar with the poem, set it up in your art center and encourage youngsters to decorate the border around the poem. Then display the finished work in your classroom.

All Kinds of Animals

All kinds of animals,
Big animals and small—
They walk and they run;
They swim and they crawl.

All kinds of animals,
Living everywhere.
They live on the land,
In the water, in the air.

All kinds of animals,
Wherever they may be,
They all need a home
Just like you and me!

Classification Station

This classification station can be tailor-made to fit the needs and abilities of your youngsters. In advance, make a supply of the animal patterns on pages 157 and 158 on construction paper. Color, laminate, and cut out the animals. Stimulate your youngsters to think in terms of various attributes by setting up your choices of the classification stations that follow.

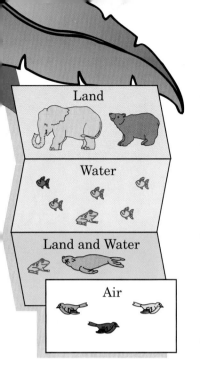

Natural Environment
To classify the animals by environment, prepare a sorting board by taping three sheets of construction paper together, leaving a small space between each sheet (for folding purposes). Label one sheet "land," another "water," and the last "land and water." Add picture cues if desired. To do this activity, have a child sort the animals according to the environments in which they live. Have spare sheets available for those youngsters who determine that some animals live in an environment that is not represented on the board. (For example, some children might suggest that birds live in the air.) Encourage youngsters to name the new categories for these animals. (If desired, color-code the animals and the environments for self-checking.)

Farm or Zoo for You?
To classify by farm or zoo animal, duplicate the farm and zoo patterns on page 159) on construction paper. Color and cut out the patterns. Then glue each pattern to a different large sheet of construction paper and laminate the pages. Encourage each child to sort the animals in the appropriate places.

Size
Cut a small, medium, and large circle from construction paper; then write the size word on each circle. Encourage children to sort the animals according to the size of the pictures. Also create a size seriation activity by having youngsters arrange an appropriate selection of the animals from smallest to largest.

Can I Keep Him?
Your little ones might get some humorous discussions going about whether or not some of these animals would be suitable for home living. For this activity, provide each child with his own set of animal patterns, a sheet of construction paper, and crayons. Have each child draw and color a picture of his home. Then encourage him to decide which of the animals might make good pets, and glue them to the scene. Some of the animal choices might be up for debate!

Travelin' Along
To classify animals according to how they travel, prepare a sorting board similar to the one described in "Natural Environment," but use four sheets of construction paper. Label the sections "walk/run," "swim," "hop/jump," and "fly." Have each child sort the animals accordingly.

Life-Size, Yikes Size!

Astonish your little ones with some life-size scientific facts about the larger members of the animal kingdom. Choose one (or more) of the animals below; then use an opaque projector to project that animal pattern from pages 157 and 158 onto a large sheet(s) of craft paper. Back up the projector until the image reaches approximate life size. Trace around the outline; then cut it out. Tape the life-size animal to a wall so that its feet are touching the floor. Invite youngsters to compare themselves with these magnificent beasts.

whale (Orca)—up to 30 feet long
elephant (African)—about 11 feet tall at the shoulder
bear (brown)—about 8 feet long
lion (male)—about 9 feet long and 3 1/2 feet tall at the shoulder

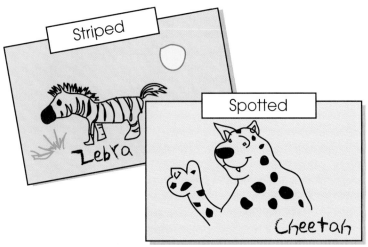

Animal Patterns and Colors

This multidisciplinary activity requires that all thinking caps be securely fastened. First title a bulletin board "Animal Patterns and Colors"; then add the labels "Stripes," "Spots," and "Colors." (Leave an open space at the bottom for those animals that need a category of their own.) Using ideas from your reading-corner books or students' imaginations, have children use various art supplies to create animals to display on the board. Assist each child in mounting his animal on the board. Then have him use those emerging reading and writing skills to write/dictate a label for his animal. Some of the trickier animals will require extra thinking. For example, is that butterfly spotted? No, it's striped! Wait—it's colored! What will your label be?

All in an Animal

If you made life-size animals in "Life-Size, Yikes Size!", you've got the perfect opportunity to cross into other areas of the curriculum with these creatures:

Measurement
Your large classroom animals are ideal for measuring activities. Provide measuring tools such as Unifix cubes, rulers, yardsticks, and construction paper paw prints. Encourage children to use the tools to explore measuring the animal(s) in different ways. For example, one child might measure the animal from nose to tail, while another measures from foot to ear. Have each child record his results on a chart.

Artistic Interpretation
During center time, invite youngsters to visit the reading corner to study the colorings and markings of the life-size animals that you made. Encourage students to look for colors as well as stripes, spots, or other interesting patterns/markings. Then line the floor below the animal cutout with newspaper and provide paints, sponges, and paintbrushes. As children rotate through centers, invite them to take turns painting your life-size animal. (If your youngsters get really inspired, you might like to have an easel-painting option available too!)

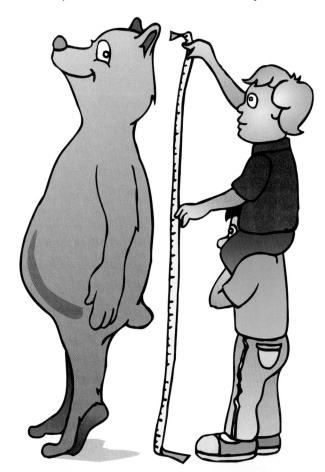

Action! Action!

Read aloud *Pretend You're a Cat* by Jean Marzollo. Before the first few words are out of your mouth, your little ones will just have to get up and get moving! For each page, choose a group of students to pantomime the text as you read aloud. Before you read the last line of each page, have the pantomiming group sit down. Then read the last line aloud and ask for volunteers to act out responses to the last line of text on each page. (If possible, videotape the readings and performances. When your youngsters watch the video, serve animal crackers.)

leap
lion
tiger
leopard
jaguar

Action Words

Build on the vocabulary of action words introduced to your youngsters in *Pretend You're a Cat*. Select one (or more) action word(s) from each animal's description. Write these words on separate sheets of chart paper. Then ask youngsters to brainstorm a list of additional animals that can move in the same way. During center time, encourage child volunteers to cut out pictures from magazines or draw to illustrate your new vocabulary charts.

Animal Big Book

After all this animal activity, your youngsters will be ready to author this big book. For each child, reproduce the big-book text on page 160 on construction paper. Have each child cut out the text, then glue it to the bottom of a large sheet of construction paper. Then encourage each child to draw the animal of his choice in the space above the text. Have each child write/dictate the animal's name in the first blank. Then ask him to suggest a *sound* word to write in the next blank, and write the animal name again in the third blank. Complete the text by having the child write an *action* word in the last blank. Bind all of the pages together. Share the book during a group reading time, and encourage your class to read the text and act it out together.

Animal Books

An Alphabet of Dinosaurs
By Peter Dodson
Illustrated by Wayne D. Barlowe

The Ocean Alphabet Book
By Jerry Pallotta
Illustrated by Frank Mazzola Jr.

The Lifesize Animal Counting Book
Published by Dorling Kindersley

Counting Cows
By Woody Jackson

Quick as a Cricket
By Audrey Wood
Illustrated by Don Wood

I pretend I'm a _lion_.
It's so fun to do!
I can _roar_
   like a _lion_.
And I can _jump_
   like one too.

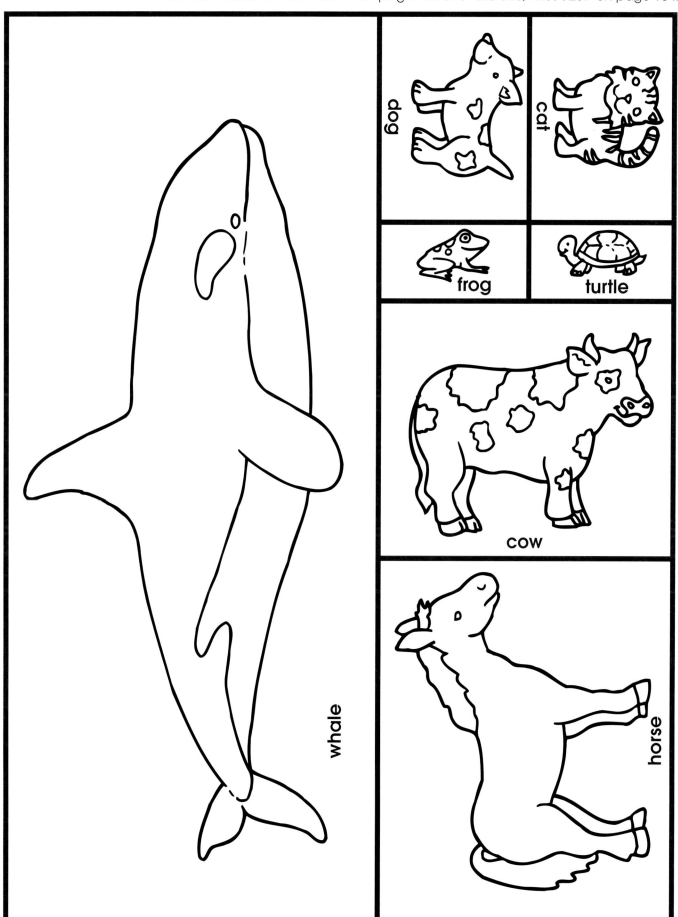

dog

cat

frog

turtle

cow

horse

whale

Animal Patterns
Use with "Classification Station" on page 153 and "Life-Size, Yikes Size!" on page 154.

elephant

lion

pig

bluebird

fish

bear

seal

I pretend I'm a _____.

It's so fun to do!

I can _____

   like a _____.

And I can _____

   like one too.

©The Mailbox® • *Science* • TEC1493

Award

I've been studying animals—
ask me to tell you about it!

©The Mailbox® • *Science* • TEC1493